ARE YOU SURE?

PETER. JUDAS. SALVATION OR DAMNATION.

BY SEBASTIAN LUCIDO

Scripture quotations are taken from the *New King James Version* of the Bible.
Copyright © 1982 by Thomas Nelson, Inc. Used by permission. All rights reserved.

Periodic Use for Key Word Definition Source
Unger's Bible Dictionary
Copyright © 1957, 1961, 1966 by
The Moody Bible Institute of Chicago

Vine's Complete Expository Dictionary of
Old and New Testament Words
Copyright © 1985 by Thomas Nelson, Inc.

ARE YOU SURE?
ISBN 978-0-692-93040-3
Copyright © 2017 by
Sebastian Lucido

Published by
Lucido Media Group LLC
www.lucidomedia.com

Acknowledgements
Jonathan Coussens, Producer
Mary Richardson, Assistant Writer
Chris Shamus (shamusdesign.com), Graphic Designer

ARE YOU SURE?

PETER. JUDAS. SALVATION OR DAMNATION.

BY SEBASTIAN LUCIDO

TABLE OF CONTENTS

SESSION 1
FALLEN AND BROKEN

FALLEN AND BROKEN

Mark 14:17-26

[17] IN THE EVENING HE CAME WITH THE TWELVE. [18] NOW AS THEY SAT AND ATE, JESUS SAID, "ASSUREDLY, I SAY TO YOU, ONE OF YOU WHO EATS WITH ME WILL BETRAY ME." [19] AND THEY BEGAN TO BE SORROWFUL, AND TO SAY TO HIM ONE BY ONE, "IS IT I?" AND ANOTHER SAID, "IS IT I?" [20] HE ANSWERED AND SAID TO THEM, "IT IS ONE OF THE TWELVE, WHO DIPS WITH ME IN THE DISH. [21] THE SON OF MAN INDEED GOES JUST AS IT IS WRITTEN OF HIM, BUT WOE TO THAT MAN BY WHOM THE SON OF MAN IS BETRAYED! IT WOULD HAVE BEEN GOOD FOR THAT MAN IF HE HAD NEVER BEEN BORN." [22] AND AS THEY WERE EATING, JESUS TOOK BREAD, BLESSED AND BROKE IT, AND GAVE IT TO THEM AND SAID, "TAKE, EAT; THIS IS MY BODY." [23] THEN HE TOOK THE CUP, AND WHEN HE HAD GIVEN THANKS HE GAVE IT TO THEM, AND THEY ALL DRANK FROM IT. [24] AND HE SAID TO THEM, "THIS IS MY BLOOD OF THE NEW COVENANT, WHICH IS SHED FOR MANY. [25] ASSUREDLY, I SAY TO YOU, I WILL NO LONGER DRINK OF THE FRUIT OF THE VINE UNTIL THAT DAY WHEN I DRINK IT NEW IN THE KINGDOM OF GOD." [26] AND WHEN THEY HAD SUNG A HYMN, THEY WENT OUT TO THE MOUNT OF OLIVES.

1. The difference in Judas was an _____ defect and Judas never _____ Jesus in his life as Lord and Savior.

2. Through Adam all of mankind became _____, _____ and _____ in the eyes of God.

3. Through Jesus man can become _____ and has _____ _____ with Him and the Father.

4. Satan's lie, "You shall not surely die," has caused man to be deceived into thinking there are no _____ for sin and God will not _____ their disobedience.

5. Satan's message is for man to have no _____ of God and no need to fear our _____ against God's Word.

6. Satan deceived Adam and Eve into believing they "will be as gods _____ right from wrong and good from evil."

7. God did not judge Adam and Eve. It was their own _____ that judged them.

8. Satan's real message to mankind through Adam is this: "You can go _____ your Creator and you don't have to glorify God as Creator or the _____ over His Creation."

9. Man dies _____ first and is reduced to a fleshly state.

10. Man's soul dies and causes man to feel _____, _____ and _____.

11. Fallen man is now more influenced by their _____, the _____ system and by the voice of _____.

12. After the fall in the Garden, _____ became man's spiritual father because of the _____ of God in man's life, and man had no way out of their _____ _____.

13. All of humanity is born _____ from God and is dead in their spirit and soul, and eventually in their _____.

14. Our salvation is _____ at the point of our physical death.

15. We are saved from the _____ and _____ of God and we are redeemed and reconciled.

16. When we _____ and disregard God's Word, we are putting ourselves _____ God.

Key Words:

(a) Salvation   (b) Awakening   (c) Body   (d) Soul   (e) Spirit

_____ Physical structure of a person; the instrument of life.

_____ Newfound awareness and resurrection from spiritual death and moral sloth.

_____ Moral and emotional nature of human beings; natural life of the body.

_____ Freely offered to all but is conditional upon repentance and faith in Christ.

_____ The invisible part of man that is related to worship and divine communion.

Session Answers:

1. internal, elevated

2. sinful, unrighteous, condemned

3. righteous, eternal life

4. consequences, judge

5. fear, actions

6. determining

7. sin

8. above, authority

9. spiritually

10. fear, shame, guilt

11. flesh, world, Satan

12. Satan, absence, fallen state

13. separated, body

14. sealed

15. wrath, judgment

16. disobey, above

Key Word Answers:

c, b, d, a, e

ETERNAL PITFALLS

Read: Mark 14

I would like for you to imagine with me the Last Supper. Not the way we have all seen the Leonardo da Vinci painting, but more like a party, with laughter and singing. Then suddenly, right in the middle of the party, Jesus interrupts it with quite the bombshell, "…one of you will betray me tonight." We all know the story. And we know the conclusions of the two apostles. Peter lived on to greatness, while Judas died in infamy. This interruption changed two men's eternal destinies. But it wasn't the interruption that determined the outcome; it was the attitude of their hearts.

Throughout Jesus' ministry, we see the actions in their hearts and the path that ultimately shaped their destinies. It's important to reflect and understand how they each came to that point and what we can do to be sure to avoid the eternal pitfalls of Judas. You see, both of them were part of the twelve who went out to minister to others, and both were there when Jesus raised Lazarus from the dead. And they were both there when Jesus walked on water.

How do you walk with Jesus and witness the greatest miracles and anointing ever, yet still fail to make it to heaven? What was the defect in Judas?

The defect had to be internal, not external, because the apostles couldn't pick Judas out of a lineup.

Over the coming weeks we are going to take a look at both Peter and Judas, and discover what allowed one to succeed and the other to fail.

Questions and Prayer:

Why do you think Jesus prayed for Peter instead of Judas? What can you do to ensure that you walk in faith like Peter? Pray today to be more like Peter. Ask for forgiveness of sin and be willing to follow Jesus in every area of your life.

DEATH OF ONE MAN

Read: Romans 5 and Romans 2

Romans 5:8-12 frames salvation for us. Salvation protects us from the judgment of God, and we become free from sin and right with God. We must understand that Jesus is the answer. It is only through His death on the cross and resurrection that we are saved.

The Bible tells us that through our faith in His body and blood we receive our salvation. If we look at Romans 5:12, we learn that there was no sin in the world, but sin came in through one man—Adam.

Salvation is the answer to the problem of Adam's first sin in the Garden. We must understand that the sin of one man, Adam, condemns all men for eternity. But the death of one man, Jesus, gives all of mankind the ability to receive salvation.

We have death through Adam and we have life through Jesus Christ. Amen.

Most of humanity believes that our actions will get us to heaven, but it is not our actions. It is our belief in the Gospel plan that allows us to receive salvation through Jesus.

The penalty of sin is death, but the gift of God is eternal life!

Questions and Prayer:

Do you recognize that salvation is the only way to heaven? Pray today that you would draw nearer to God as you come into a deeper understanding of salvation.

GOD AS CREATOR

Read: Genesis 3

The ultimate lie from Satan is that you would be as gods, determining what is right and wrong and what is good and evil for yourself. Satan's propaganda is that you will be like God.

When you take a broader look at it, he is really saying to not fear God and not fear the consequences of disobeying Him, and then you will be as a god.

Satan's lie is that you don't need to glorify God as Creator and you don't need to respect God's authority over His creation to determine right from wrong. Satan is telling men and women that they can go above and disregard their Creator. He is saying we can use His creation as we see fit because we are the gods of our environment.

All sin comes from this thinking process, whether it is through our ignorance or knowledge. When we disobey God's Word with or without intent, we are putting ourselves above the Creator. We are putting ourselves above His authority to determine what is right and wrong, and above His authority to judge His creation. This dangerous thinking puts us in the position of using and abusing His creation.

Questions and Prayer:

Are there areas of your life that you have not allowed God to take full control? Are there areas that you don't trust God with? Today, ask God to forgive you of holding onto those areas and submit them to Him. Allow Him to be God in your life.

NO LONGER IN HARMONY

Read: Genesis 3:6-8

It is interesting to see in these verses that God did not judge Adam and Eve personally after they sinned. He could have. In fact, He could have walked into the Garden of Eden and immediately destroyed them for their disobedience. He could have tossed them straight into hell, but He didn't. Instead, because of His immeasurable love for them, He allowed them to live and He developed a plan for their salvation. Their sin, however, was not without consequences. But remember, it was their sin that brought about the consequences, not God.

Why? What happened?

When Adam and Eve saw their nakedness, they felt guilt and shame, and their environment immediately changed.

This is the fall of man. Mankind spiritually died and became unrighteous. In other words, mankind was no longer in harmony with God. As a result, Adam, Eve and ultimately all of mankind died spiritually. Their hearts became infected. Their minds changed. Their bodies became mortal.

Adam and Eve experienced the same emotions and struggles we experience today. They felt depressed, had low self-esteem and experienced fear. They wanted to hide and cover their dishonor. They wanted to cover their guilt. This was not there before in their lives. But everything changed in their environment and they were separated from their Creator. Sadly, they were reduced to what we know as "the human condition," and their spirits were in need of salvation.

Questions and Prayer:

How often do you experience fear, depression, loss of self-worth, or shame as a result of sin? Once you believe and accept the salvation of God, these emotions are reduced in both thought and action. Today, pray that God would reveal His salvation to you in your mind, your spirit and your emotions.

VOID OF GOD

Read: Ephesians 2

Today, there are over 7 billion people living on the earth, and most of them are walking in spiritual death. The majority, from newborn baby to the most powerful politician, is spiritually dead. God is completely absent from their minds and they have no relationship with Him. And the Bible tells us the decisions being made by mankind are without any regard to God.

The Bible says that humanity is moved by the "power of the prince of the air," which is Satan. We are told that Satan's influence has become dominate in humanity because of the absence of a relationship with God. Satan's voice is more familiar to us than God's voice.

So, when you look at mankind's three parts (spirit, soul and body), and when we were alive to God, His spirit dominated the presence of who we were on the earth. Adam's spirit is what drove him because his relationship with God was direct and spiritual. When Adam fell, his spirit died and he was not alive to God.

Adam was reduced to his soul and mind, which are his will, intellect, memory, reasoning and body. Now, mankind is driven by their five senses and whatever gives them pleasure. We build moral boundaries in our lives, but those boundaries are not God's boundaries. Mankind makes decisions based on being disconnected from God. When you put all of this together, you have the human race, racing away from the things of God.

Satan is the voice of the atheist, the agnostic, the Buddhist and the Muslim. He is the voice of all groups, whether religious or social, that are not of God. When you look at the world, humanity is completely lost because the earth is void of God, except for those who have had an awakening and find salvation.

Questions and Prayer:

Is God's voice alive in you? What's influencing your decisions? Pray today that you are influenced by and influencing others with His voice, not the voice of the evil one.

GOD'S CONTRACT TO FIX OUR PROBLEM

SESSION 2
GOD'S CONTRACT TO FIX OUR PROBLEM

Hebrews 10:9-21

[9] THEN HE SAID, "BEHOLD, I HAVE COME TO DO YOUR WILL, O GOD." HE TAKES AWAY THE FIRST THAT HE MAY ESTABLISH THE SECOND. [10] BY THAT WILL WE HAVE BEEN SANCTIFIED THROUGH THE OFFERING OF THE BODY OF JESUS CHRIST ONCE FOR ALL. [11] AND EVERY PRIEST STANDS MINISTERING DAILY AND OFFERING REPEATEDLY THE SAME SACRIFICES, WHICH CAN NEVER TAKE AWAY SINS. [12] BUT THIS MAN, AFTER HE HAD OFFERED ONE SACRIFICE FOR SINS FOREVER, SAT DOWN AT THE RIGHT HAND OF GOD, [13] FROM THAT TIME WAITING TILL HIS ENEMIES ARE MADE HIS FOOTSTOOL. [14] FOR BY ONE OFFERING HE HAS PERFECTED FOREVER THOSE WHO ARE BEING SANCTIFIED. [15] BUT THE HOLY SPIRIT ALSO WITNESSES TO US; FOR AFTER HE HAD SAID BEFORE, [16] "THIS IS THE COVENANT THAT I WILL MAKE WITH THEM AFTER THOSE DAYS, SAYS THE LORD: I WILL PUT MY LAWS INTO THEIR HEARTS, AND IN THEIR MINDS I WILL WRITE THEM," [17] THEN HE ADDS, "THEIR SINS AND THEIR LAWLESS DEEDS I WILL REMEMBER NO MORE." [18] NOW WHERE THERE IS REMISSION OF THESE, THERE IS NO LONGER AN OFFERING FOR SIN. [19] THEREFORE, BRETHREN, HAVING BOLDNESS TO ENTER THE HOLIEST BY THE BLOOD OF JESUS, [20] BY A NEW AND LIVING WAY WHICH HE CONSECRATED FOR US, THROUGH THE VEIL, THAT IS, HIS FLESH, [21] AND HAVING A HIGH PRIEST OVER THE HOUSE OF GOD.

1.   A covenant is an _____ that is stronger than family or _____.

2.   The _____ and rituals of the covenant agreement represent God reaching out and _____ Himself to man.

3.   A covenant can be between two people, families, a _____ or nations. The representative of each is called the _____.

4.   A covenant agreement goes beyond _____ because it is passed on through the _____.

5.   The signs or seals of a covenant are:

a)   A _____ or death and then walking between the sacrificed pieces signifies "one forever."

b) Cutting the wrist or hand and _____ hands mingles the blood. This represents a mixing of the blood, meaning, what is in me is now in you.

c) Exchange of a _____. This proclaims I will _____ you with my life both in offense and defense.

d) An exchange of a _____. This gives you the same position and _____ that I have within my own group.

e) Exchange or change of a _____. This gives you power of attorney to transact business in my family, tribe or nation.

f) The _____ of the covenant agreement are an outline of the vows and _____ as well as the curses if the covenant is broken.

g) A covenant _____ is celebrated with bread and wine. This is done between the covenant partners.

6. _____ means to dip or submerge into something else so that the object takes on a new identity. An example is when a white garment is dipped into blue dye; it becomes blue.

7. New Testament terms that signify we are in covenant with Jesus are: _____ Him, _____ Him, _____ Him, _____ Him, or _____ Christ or _____ Jesus, so on and so forth.

8. When we are in covenant with God we lack nothing and we are _____ in Christ.

9. God promises a new and _____ covenant that established an _____ fix through salvation. Our salvation would bring _____ and undo the problem between God and _____.

10. The Bible is divided into the Old Testament or the _____ _____ and the New Testament or the _____ _____.

11. The _____ accomplished something, but the new is better. The old priesthood was good, but the new _____ is much, much better.

Key Words:

(a) Vows   (b) Covenant   (c) Blood Brothers   (d) Holy of Holies   (e) Power of Attorney

_____ Signed written agreement that binds two parties or nations together.

_____ Inner chamber of the tabernacle reserved for the presence of God.

_____ Solemn promise, pledge or personal commitment.

_____ Authority to act in place of another person according to contract agreement.

_____ Individuals who vow mutual fidelity and trust by mingling each other's blood.

Session Answers:

1. agreement, nations

2. seals, binding

3. tribe, mediator

4. generations, bloodline

5a. sacrifice

5b. shaking

5c. weapon, defend

5d. robe, authority

5e. name

5f. terms, blessings

5g. meal

6. Baptism

7. in, with, by, through, in, in

8. complete

9. everlasting, eternal, life, mankind

10. Old Covenant, New Covenant

11. old, Priesthood

Key Word Answers:

b, d, a, e, c

BOUND BY COVENANT

Read: Hebrews 10

Hebrews 10 talks about the New Covenant. In fact, it goes into detail regarding the covenant—or contract and agreement—that God made with mankind.

What is a covenant?

A covenant is a contract or agreement between two parties. It can be between two people, two families, two tribes or even two nations. We have contracts and agreements in civilized America today. But if we go back in history, even to when we first came to North America, people were living in uncivilized areas based on covenants. You have probably heard the term "blood brothers," and this is where Native Americans would cut covenants and make agreements. Tribes would make agreements with one another by binding themselves in an unbreakable bond that was sealed in blood. We do not see that today because essentially, we sign an agreement on paper in the hopes that each party will keep their word. But this is the way that people lived all over the world for many years.

A covenant is more binding than family; it is more binding than your nation. It is the most binding agreement that a person can ever make. The closest thing we have today is the marriage covenant when a man and a woman choose to be one. They choose to merge their lives and make an agreement together in a covenant relationship. When a person, tribe or nation binds themselves to another in covenant, it is not something they would do haphazardly, because it is unbreakable. A covenant is something that you bind yourself to for life.

Questions and Prayer:

Have you ever made a covenant with someone? Have you kept that agreement, or did you haphazardly break it? Pray today that God would show you the areas of your life where you could enter into covenant with Him.

BEYOND GENERATIONS

Read: Genesis 15

God made a covenant with Abraham. Today, we will explore the meaning of covenant and the different types of covenants that exist.

Animal Covenant: An animal covenant was a common covenant in ancient times. One would take an animal and split it headlong. Yes, this sounds odd today, but in ancient times we would split the animal and lay the pieces side-by-side. Then, we would walk through the pieces in a figure eight. This would be similar to an infinity sign, and it meant that we are one forever. During this ritual, we would say aloud, "We are now one, forever."

Blood Covenant: Another type of covenant is a blood covenant. Here, we would cut our hand or wrist and combine blood. This is where we get the greeting of a handshake, but in ancient times they would mingle their blood. This handshake means that what is in me is now in you and what is in you is now in me. And this covenant agreement goes beyond generations, because the agreement would pass through the bloodline. By sealing the agreement in blood, they are telling one another that not them but their heirs are bound to each another because of this covenant.

Weapon Covenant: Another type of covenant is a weapon covenant. One would exchange a weapon with another. I would take my sword, my bow or my gun and give it to you, and then you would give yours to me. This meant I am going to defend you with my life. Then, if someone attacks you, they will be attacking me. It was a symbol that we will always be there to defend each other. Oftentimes, a weaker tribe would go to a larger tribe or nation and bind themselves together so the weaker tribe would have greater protection. Today, we have a similar agreement in NATO and the United Nations. In essence, if you attack one nation, all the nations are being attacked.

Questions and Prayer:

What kind of covenants or promises have you made with others? Have you been loyal to those promises? Make a covenant to God today to be His forever, to defend His name, and to teach the next generation about His grace and salvation.

PERSONAL DEVOTION SESSION 2 // DAY 3

POWER OF ATTORNEY

Read: 2 Samuel 7

In 2 Samuel 7, God made a covenant with David. Today, let's discover its significance and the aspects of the marriage covenant that existed in ancient times and today.

Robe Covenant: A robe covenant is a covenant that still exists today, such as our covenant of marriage where we exchange rings. However, in ancient times they would exchange a robe, because a robe or article of clothing determined who you were. If I was a prince and you wore my robe, that would mean you were a prince in my nation. Many times this happened through marriage. For example, a certain king's son would marry another king's daughter and there would be an exchange. Robes were used in covenant even in the Bible. Think about how Paul said, "…when we took the robe of the righteousness of Jesus." Paul is explaining how we exchanged our filthy rags, shame and guilt with the robe of Jesus, the Son of God.

In a robe covenant there is also the exchange of a name, which represents a type of power of attorney. Think of how in a marriage the two come together and their properties are now the same. They also have power of attorney to make transactions in one another's names. Meaning I could go into your grain warehouse if I needed wheat or food for my country, because you promised to feed me and, likewise, you could do the same.

Part of the covenant process would include a covenant feast or meal with bread and wine. During the meal we would go over the vows and promises. These promises would include defense, protection, possessions and unity.

Salvation is the ultimate covenant. Like a marriage, salvation is a coming together because it is a relationship, and it is a covenant agreement between the two.

Questions and Prayer:

Have you ever thought of yourself as being married to Christ? What does that mean to you? What are your responsibilities in that marriage? Ask God to reveal how you can become a better partner in your relationship with Him.

IDENTIFIED WITH HIM

Read: Colossians 2

In the New Testament, any time you see the covenant terms in Him, in Jesus, with Jesus, through Jesus, through Him, or with Him, it means you are connected to Him. We quickly gloss over these terms, but they mean everything to us! The Bible says in Colossians 2:10 "…you are complete in Him." That is because on our own, we are not complete; but in Him, we are complete—with nothing lacking in us. We know who we are and we're growing into who we're supposed to be. We are complete in Him because of the covenant that God made between Himself and Jesus, and then, Jesus made between Himself and us.

It is not a physical covenant but a spiritual covenant. The Bible says that by faith in God's Gospel plan, you are joined into the covenant and are identified with Jesus in His death, burial and resurrection.

It is through faith in God's plan that we become a participant in this unbreakable covenant. We call that baptism, or baptizo. It is like the dying of a garment. If you were to take a white garment and immerse it in blue dye, the white garment becomes blue and is identified by the blue dye. It is no longer a white garment. This is baptism.

When we come into covenant with God, we are complete in Christ and become spiritually alive. We are changed from whatever we were to what He desires us to be.

Questions and Prayer:

Have you ever seen yourself as completely transformed? Think about who you were and who you are now in God's eyes. Ask Him today to give you revelation on how you have become a new creation in His eyes, and to show you how He sees you as being complete in Him.

PERSONAL DEVOTION SESSION 2 // DAY 5

THE ROYAL ROBE

Read: Hebrews 10:18-22

The Old Testament Temple had an outer court and an inner court, and within the inner court was the Holiest of Holies. Within the Holiest of Holies was the Ark of the Covenant and the presence of God. A veil blocked the Ark, and only the high priest could enter this area on behalf of the people to make a temporary sacrifice for their sins.

In Hebrews 10, we read about our New Covenant in Jesus. Now we can go into the Holiest of Holies and enter into the presence of God. Why can we now enter? Because we are spiritually alive in Christ. We have been made holy and righteous in God's sight.

God made a covenant with Jesus. In turn, Jesus made a covenant with humanity. This is why we can go into God's presence and enjoy a direct relationship with Him. We learn in John 16:23, that we don't have to ask Jesus for anything; instead, we can directly ask the Father in the name of Jesus.

Now when you look through the Bible, you will start to see all of these different covenant terms that feed back into the contractual arrangement of salvation through Jesus.

Today, the righteousness we have been given in Christ is the royal robe of Jesus. Jesus took off His robe and gave it to us. He covered us. He made a covenant with us! He took on our filth, our shame, and our sin upon Himself. This was all done through the covenant He made with humanity.

Questions and Prayer:

When was the last time you went to God for something? Perhaps it was for forgiveness? Today, go to God as His child and ask Him to reveal to you His love for you, as He loves Jesus.

SESSION 3
GRACE - A GIFT FROM HEAVEN

GRACE - A GIFT FROM HEAVEN

Isaiah 53:1-12

[1] WHO HAS BELIEVED OUR REPORT? AND TO WHOM HAS THE ARM OF THE LORD BEEN REVEALED? [2] FOR HE SHALL GROW UP BEFORE HIM AS A TENDER PLANT, AND AS A ROOT OUT OF DRY GROUND. HE HAS NO FORM OR COMELINESS; AND WHEN WE SEE HIM, THERE IS NO BEAUTY THAT WE SHOULD DESIRE HIM. [3] HE IS DESPISED AND REJECTED BY MEN, A MAN OF SORROWS AND ACQUAINTED WITH GRIEF. AND WE HID, AS IT WERE, OUR FACES FROM HIM; HE WAS DESPISED, AND WE DID NOT ESTEEM HIM. [4] SURELY HE HAS BORNE OUR GRIEFS AND CARRIED OUR SORROWS; YET WE ESTEEMED HIM STRICKEN, SMITTEN BY GOD, AND AFFLICTED. [5] BUT HE WAS WOUNDED FOR OUR TRANSGRESSIONS, HE WAS BRUISED FOR OUR INIQUITIES; THE CHASTISEMENT FOR OUR PEACE WAS UPON HIM, AND BY HIS STRIPES WE ARE HEALED. [6] ALL WE LIKE SHEEP HAVE GONE ASTRAY; WE HAVE TURNED, EVERY ONE, TO HIS OWN WAY; AND THE LORD HAS LAID ON HIM THE INIQUITY OF US ALL. [7] HE WAS OPPRESSED AND HE WAS AFFLICTED, YET HE OPENED NOT HIS MOUTH; HE WAS LED AS A LAMB TO THE SLAUGHTER, AND AS A SHEEP BEFORE ITS SHEARERS IS SILENT, SO HE OPENED NOT HIS MOUTH. [8] HE WAS TAKEN FROM PRISON AND FROM JUDGMENT, AND WHO WILL DECLARE HIS GENERATION? FOR HE WAS CUT OFF FROM THE LAND OF THE LIVING; FOR THE TRANSGRESSIONS OF MY PEOPLE HE WAS STRICKEN. [9] AND THEY MADE HIS GRAVE WITH THE WICKED-- BUT WITH THE RICH AT HIS DEATH, BECAUSE HE HAD DONE NO VIOLENCE, NOR WAS ANY DECEIT IN HIS MOUTH. [10] YET IT PLEASED THE LORD TO BRUISE HIM; HE HAS PUT HIM TO GRIEF. WHEN YOU MAKE HIS SOUL AN OFFERING FOR SIN, HE SHALL SEE HIS SEED, HE SHALL PROLONG HIS DAYS, AND THE PLEASURE OF THE LORD SHALL PROSPER IN HIS HAND. [11] HE SHALL SEE THE LABOR OF HIS SOUL, AND BE SATISFIED. BY HIS KNOWLEDGE MY RIGHTEOUS SERVANT SHALL JUSTIFY MANY, FOR HE SHALL BEAR THEIR INIQUITIES. [12] THEREFORE I WILL DIVIDE HIM A PORTION WITH THE GREAT, AND HE SHALL DIVIDE THE SPOIL WITH THE STRONG, BECAUSE HE POURED OUT HIS SOUL UNTO DEATH, AND HE WAS NUMBERED WITH THE TRANSGRESSORS, AND HE BORE THE SIN OF MANY, AND MADE INTERCESSION FOR THE TRANSGRESSORS.

1.	Grace is unmerited favor and it is a _____ from God. Jesus Christ is the _____ of God given to humanity.

2.   We were given the gift of Jesus Christ by God, and through _____ we have salvation.

3.   God presents us with a door of salvation but we have to _____ with God and put our faith into action by _____ through the door.

4.   The beneficiary who _____ this gift did not earn it or work for it because a gift is _____ given. Grace is difficult for humanity to understand because our nature is _____ _____.

5.   We see _____ and _____ working together when David brought Mephibosheth back into his kingdom.

6.   To be _____ is to be in right standing with God. Man was _____ and separated from God because of Adam's fall in the Garden.

7.   All men and women are _____ unrighteous and are in need of _____. Therefore, no one in _____ could fix our unrighteousness, so God planned for a fix—His Son, Jesus Christ.

8.   An _____ person is unrighteous and a _____ person is righteous.

9.   Everything God did toward Jesus was _____ to give us salvation. Jesus has no sin or _____ _____, allowing Him to be perfect because He was born in God's image.

10.   God put all of our past, present and future sin on Jesus and this is called the _____ work of Jesus. It is where God put Jesus in _____ _____.

11.   Jesus came into this world as a perfect _____ for the sacrifice of mankind. The cross satisfied the _____ _____ _____ and the requirements that are on God the Father to us.

12.   Believers are the beneficiary of grace because we have been _____ through Christ's body and made clean by His _____ to the Father.

Key Words:

(a) Righteousness   (b) Justified   (c) Substitutional   (d) Beneficiary   (e) Sanctified

_____ Someone who gains an advantage or profits from something.

_____ State of moral obedience required by God to enter into heaven.

_____ Separation process of the believer from evil things and ways.

_____ When God declares those who place their faith in Christ to be righteous.

_____ Action of replacing someone with another person.

Session Answers:

1. gift, grace

2. faith

3. cooperate, walking

4. receives, freely, works based

5. covenant, grace

6. righteous, unrighteous

7. born, salvation, humanity

8. unsaved, saved

9. necessary, sin nature

10. substitutional, our place

11. Lamb, court of heaven

12. sanctified, sacrifice

Key Word Answers:

d, a, e, b, c

RECOGNIZE JESUS

Read: Matthew 26

Mary of Bethany was a woman who stood head and shoulders above the rest. Every time the Bible mentions Mary of Bethany we learn that she is at the feet of Jesus. She was at His feet when He was teaching. Everyone remembers the story of Mary and Martha. Martha was serving while Mary was listening and learning from the Teacher. Jesus corrected Martha for being busy, but praised Mary for her devotion.

When Mary's brother, Lazarus, died she came again to Jesus. Then in Matthew, we learn that she saved a year's worth of wages, and bought precious ointment. She knew that Jesus was going to die and she saved that ointment for His burial. When she poured the ointment on the feet of Jesus, the Bible tells us that some of the disciples were indignant and asked why it was not sold and given to the poor. We learn in John's gospel that it was Judas who led the revolt.

Jesus scolds the disciples and pleads with them to recognize Him as who He really is. He goes on to say in Matthew 26:11, "For you have the poor with you always, but Me you do not have always." Mary saw who Jesus was and valued Him as the Messiah, the Savior, but Judas did not. In fact, Judas never got the message. He never understood the true value of Jesus in his heart and ultimately, Judas betrayed Jesus.

Questions and Prayer:

Do you value Jesus for who He is? How do you express this value on a daily basis? Ask God today to open your eyes and soften your heart to Jesus. Ask Him to continue to reveal the value of salvation and to make you like a "Mary," removing any trace of Judas within you.

FOR BY GRACE

Read: Ephesians 2:4-10

We learned many covenant terms last week, and this week we will learn about the term "by grace".

God's motive is mercy and grace, and we read in Ephesians 2:8, "For by grace you have been saved…"

Let me explain that grace is a gift. It is the unmerited favor of God and cannot be earned. Grace is given to us even when we're not looking for it. Grace is a one-sided gift, and not something that we can earn. Again, grace is God's gift to us.

We were given the gift of Jesus Christ by God the Father, and through faith, we have salvation. Our salvation is cooperating with God and receiving the gift. The truth is it's all about cooperation. God presents us with a door of salvation, but we have to cooperate and walk in.

God's gift of grace was given to humanity so that whosoever believes in Him will find salvation and not perish (John 3:15). Jesus Christ is our salvation. God made a way where all of creation, including you and me, could be saved without His laws and statues being broken.

Questions and Prayer:

What does grace mean to you? How do you live in His grace and receive it every day? Today, pray in faith that you will receive and understand God's greatest gift through Jesus.

A RIGHTEOUS JUDGE

Read: Romans 3:21-24

I am going to define the terms of these verses as we go through them. The first term "righteousness" means right standing with God. "Unrighteousness" means that you are not in good standing with God. An unsaved person is unrighteous. A saved person is righteous.

The term "justified" means a person has been judged and found not guilty. Your case is stamped justified and the matter is closed. For God to be just in His actions while maintaining His holiness and righteousness, He had to be just in what He did to satisfy His heavenly court and laws.

God justifies this from the scrutiny of any fallen angel or other creation, or even His own laws. Everything God allowed to happen to Jesus in Scripture was necessary to gain us salvation.

People ask how God can send people to hell when they do not know Him. As Christians, we have to tell these people that God is a righteous Judge who is just in all He does. If it was necessary for Jesus to come to earth and suffer, then it was necessary in God's heavenly court.

If there was any other possible way to save humanity, I am certain God would have chosen another path. But Jesus had to go through this process in order for those who believe in Him to be saved.

Questions and Prayer:

Do you see yourself as righteous and justified? Do you battle with guilt, condemnation or fear? Why do you suppose that is? Pray today that God would reveal to you the new nature you have received by salvation.

JESUS PAID THE PRICE

Read: Isaiah 53:1-13

In this chapter of Isaiah there are three different entities. There is God the Father, Jesus Christ, and humanity. In the first verse, we learn that Jesus was a common man, or average. For all general purposes, He was ordinary looking and fit in with all of humanity. Verse four begins with what is called the "Substitutional Work of Jesus," and there we learn where God put Jesus in our place. You can put your name in these verses.

Here are two examples from Isaiah 53:4-5:

Surely Jesus has borne (_____) griefs and carried (_____) sorrows.

He was wounded for (_____) transgressions.

While Jesus was on the cross, the skies became dark as all of humanities past, present and future sins were laid upon Him. Jesus became separated from God and from eternity past. At this point, He died spiritually as a man.

Verse 8 tell us, "For He was cut off from the land of the living…" All of mankind's sin had been put on this Holy, just, sinless and blameless Lamb that God provided.

Again, use yourself as an example here. When you look at your sins—past, present and future— recognize that God has forgiven you because of the blood of Jesus. Remember, all of your sins were put on Him.

The penalty we deserved, He took. He was substituted in for us. This is the grace of God. Jesus is the grace of God. Jesus paid the penalty, both physically and spiritually. He paid our debt.

Questions and Prayer:

Do you see how Jesus was substituted in for you? What are the things in your own life that He paid for? Pray today to have a deeper understanding of the "Substitutional Work of Jesus."

BENEFICIARY OF GRACE

Read: Hebrews 10:5-10

Jesus came into this world for one purpose only: to become the sacrifice for us and pay the penalty of our sins. It was one purpose with one focus. Jesus satisfied the requirements in the court of heaven and the requirements for forgiveness of mankind's sin.

Believers are the beneficiary of this great grace. We have been sanctified and made clean by the offering of His body and blood as a sacrifice to the Father. The grace of the Father is that Jesus paid the price for us.

The Bible tells us Jesus could have called legions of angels to deliver Him when He was arrested, but He walked freely into this sacrifice. Jesus Christ is the only human ever to pick who His father and mother would be, and really even what His name would be, right?

Jesus went into the sacrifice knowing exactly what was going to happen. He knew and accepted the price to be paid for humanity's salvation ahead of time.

When we go through something traumatic we go through it once as the difficulties are happening. Jesus, however, saw His death beforehand. He wrote about it and deeply understood it, yet He went into it freely.

Through Jesus accomplishing the substitutional plan, we are sons and daughters of God. We now have rights and an inheritance through Jesus. We have protection and defense through Jesus. We have eternal life through Jesus!

This is grace!

Questions and Prayer:

What other things do you now have through the sacrifice of Jesus? Thank God for all those things!

REVELATION KNOWLEDGE

REVELATION KNOWLEDGE

1 Corinthians 2:6-14

[6] HOWEVER, WE SPEAK WISDOM AMONG THOSE WHO ARE MATURE, YET NOT THE WISDOM OF THIS AGE, NOR OF THE RULERS OF THIS AGE, WHO ARE COMING TO NOTHING. [7] BUT WE SPEAK THE WISDOM OF GOD IN A MYSTERY, THE HIDDEN WISDOM WHICH GOD ORDAINED BEFORE THE AGES FOR OUR GLORY, [8] WHICH NONE OF THE RULERS OF THIS AGE KNEW; FOR HAD THEY KNOWN, THEY WOULD NOT HAVE CRUCIFIED THE LORD OF GLORY. [9] BUT AS IT IS WRITTEN: "EYE HAS NOT SEEN, NOR EAR HEARD, NOR HAVE ENTERED INTO THE HEART OF MAN THE THINGS WHICH GOD HAS PREPARED FOR THOSE WHO LOVE HIM." [10] BUT GOD HAS REVEALED THEM TO US THROUGH HIS SPIRIT. FOR THE SPIRIT SEARCHES ALL THINGS, YES, THE DEEP THINGS OF GOD. [11] FOR WHAT MAN KNOWS THE THINGS OF A MAN EXCEPT THE SPIRIT OF THE MAN WHICH IS IN HIM? EVEN SO NO ONE KNOWS THE THINGS OF GOD EXCEPT THE SPIRIT OF GOD. [12] NOW WE HAVE RECEIVED, NOT THE SPIRIT OF THE WORLD, BUT THE SPIRIT WHO IS FROM GOD, THAT WE MIGHT KNOW THE THINGS THAT HAVE BEEN FREELY GIVEN TO US BY GOD. [13] THESE THINGS WE ALSO SPEAK, NOT IN WORDS WHICH MAN'S WISDOM TEACHES BUT WHICH THE HOLY SPIRIT TEACHES, COMPARING SPIRITUAL THINGS WITH SPIRITUAL. [14] BUT THE NATURAL MAN DOES NOT RECEIVE THE THINGS OF THE SPIRIT OF GOD, FOR THEY ARE FOOLISHNESS TO HIM; NOR CAN HE KNOW THEM, BECAUSE THEY ARE SPIRITUALLY DISCERNED.

1. Revelation is _____ knowledge or wisdom that we did not know or see. The absence or prevention of revelation is _____ or ignorance.

2. The Spirit of God reveals things in our _____, which is the same as our _____ because the heart and the spirit of a person is where revelation takes place.

3. The things of God are _____ to someone when their heart is not open to receive revelation knowledge.

4. God is always _____ to us and willing to reveal things, but we must _____ with an open heart.

5. Our hearts _____ the Word of God, and then we believe by faith and _____ what is in our hearts. Our hearts must be _____ to the revelation that Jesus is our Savior.

6. Man's heart or spirit is either _____ to receive the things of God or it is not. To have an open heart is to have faith.

7. When we receive revelation knowledge we _____ ourselves and _____ Jesus.

8. The things of God are not _____ to man. We cannot inherently know them because they are _____.

9. What the _____ tells us about God is how we know Him because the Bible is the _____ and Word of God.

10. When we realize the big picture and understand that we are not the center of the universe, we _____ all and _____ Him.

11. God is the _____ and authority over His creation, and He _____ the hand of man into writing the Bible. If you believe that God is the Creator of the universe, you must believe that He can write a _____.

12. All revelation, knowledge and understanding given to us must be _____ by His Word because anything else or any other _____ is dangerous.

13. God does not give us more _____ because we have more knowledge. And God does not give us more _____ because we have more knowledge. We walk in the grace and peace that is already available to us.

Key Words:

(a) Creation   (b) Foolishness   (c) Partake   (d) Darkness   (e) Forsake

_____ Cooperating in the activity of the Gospel message.

_____ Lack of common sense and perception to the reality of things, both natural and spiritual.

_____ Work of God in bringing into existence the universe out of nothing.

_____ Give up something formerly held dear; to renounce something.

_____ Sinful condition of moral or spiritual depravity.

Session Answers:

1. exposing, darkness

2. spirit, heart

3. foolishness

4. speaking, listen

5. receive, confess, awakened

6. open

7. humble, exalt

8. natural, hidden

9. Bible, wisdom

10. forsake, follow

11. Creator, moved, Book

12. verified, source

13. grace, peace

Key Word Answers:

c, b, a, e, d

UPON THIS ROCK

Read: Matthew 16

There are two distinct and separate stories within Matthew 16 about the Apostle Peter that I'll paraphrase for you. We see Jesus walking with His disciples and asking them what the people are saying about Him? "Who do they say I am?" They told Him that some say He is John the Baptist and others say He is Elijah or one of the prophets. But Jesus asked who do you guys (the disciples) say that I am? Peter, always willing to raise his hand and move first, replied, "You are the Christ, You are the Son of God. You are the One we are waiting for, and You are the Messiah." This is a confession of faith.

Jesus gives Peter a star and a compliment and then tells him that flesh and blood did not discern that, but God revealed it to him. Flesh and blood represents Peter himself. Jesus said, "…and on this rock I will build My church." (Matthew 16:18). The rock represents the confession of faith in Jesus Christ as the Son of God, our Lord and Savior. So it is upon that rock of the confession in the heart of mankind that God would build the Church.

In the same chapter, Jesus tells the apostles of the Gospel plan and how He has to be crucified, but will rise on the third day. Well, think about this. Peter just said that he would not let that happen to Jesus, right? Peter told Jesus that he would never let them crucify Him. Jesus then tells Peter, "Get behind me, Satan!" This is because Peter was listening to the voice of Satan instead of God's voice.

We learn here in Scripture that God reveals to us His wisdom and revelation knowledge. But I want you to understand that there is another voice, as we discussed in earlier sessions. We know that after the Fall, Satan's voice became more normal to us. It's his spiritual voice that makes more sense to us and has more influence over us. Only by activating our faith and learning to hear God's voice are we able to discern between the two voices.

Questions and Prayer:

Are you able to discern between the two voices? When was there a time you knew you heard from God? How do you overcome doubt? Pray today that God would continue to speak to you and that you would know His voice in an intimate way.

THINGS OF GOD

Read: 1 Corinthians 2

I want to go back through these verses and point out that Paul talks about the hidden wisdom and the mystery of God four times. The things of God are not natural to mankind because mankind cannot naturally know the things of God. They have to be revealed to us by God. We can see an intelligent design by God and we can see that God exists. We can see that there is a God and we can formulate that concept in our natural minds and with our senses. But we will never know or understand the things of God without Him revealing those things to us. We can't see God, we can't touch God, we can't feel God, and we can't smell God with our five natural senses because our senses cannot engage with Him. In fact, the only things we know about God is what the Bible tells us, because everything else is made up by us. What the Bible tells us about God is how we know Him, because the Bible is the wisdom and the Word of God.

Mankind on their own cannot naturally discern, know or understand the things of God.

The reason these were hidden from us was because of our spiritual death. They were hidden because we did not have a relationship with God.

This is the starting point. It is by believing God is the Creator—the Creator who has authority over His creation. He has the ability through the eons to move the hand of man into writing a Book. We have to look to the Word to learn who He is, how He thinks, how He acts, how He judges, and what He would like us to do. The Bible tells us how God wants us to live as men and a women, husband and wife, or teacher.

The Bible explains how He wants us to raise our children and how He wants us to interact with one another. All the revelation of what God has for us is written within its pages. There is the beginning in the book of Genesis, and the end is told to us in the book of Revelation. God has given us His written Word.

Questions and Prayer:

What are some ways you can know God on a deeper level? How does God speak to you? Pray today that you would have a desire to gain a deeper understanding of Him, and a desire to read and study His Word.

OPEN YOUR HEART

Read: Matthew 13

In Matthew 16, how did Peter learn Jesus was the Christ? God revealed it to Peter in his heart. As Peter walked with Jesus, he was able to see and comprehend things. Peter then knew that Jesus was the Son of God.

But what happened to Judas? He saw the same miracles and heard the same teachings. He was in the same boat when Jesus walked on the water. You see, we can experience miracle after miracle because Judas saw all the same things Peter did. Yet things were not revealed to Judas as they were to Peter. Why is that? It is because the heart of Judas was closed and therefore, he did not see things as Peter saw them.

In Matthew 13, Jesus tells us that there are two groups of people. One group is given to know the things of the Kingdom of God, and the other group is not.

Why is this other group unable to digest the message? Jesus brings it back to the heart, or the spirit of man. That is the key we have to learn. You see, the Spirit of God reveals things to us in our spirits, not in our heads. There is a difference between the head and the heart. Some of the apostles and disciples could not understand what Jesus was saying, while those who did wondered why the others could not see things clearly. Jesus told them it was because their hearts were dull of hearing.

When we see that someone is closed off and rejecting the truth, it is our job to preach the Gospel and to teach the Gospel message. But not everyone is going to receive the good news of Christ because not everyone's heart is open to the message.

Questions and Prayer:

Do you know someone who is closed to the message of the Gospel? How can you open their heart to it? Pray for their heart today, that it would be softened and opened to the truth.

GRACE AND PEACE

Read: 2 Peter 1

We learn in 2 Peter 1:2 that grace and peace are multiplied through the knowledge of God. The Bible says that grace is God's unmerited gift of Jesus Christ and peace is the tranquility of the soul. These are multiplied to us, expanded unto us, through revelation knowledge. Please pay close attention here, because God does not give us more grace just because we have more knowledge. And God does not give us more peace just because we have more knowledge. We walk in the grace and peace that is already available to us.

Of course, God answers prayers and brings grace and peace into your life. Meanwhile, you walk in expanding grace and peace in your life because you have revelation knowledge. With revelation knowledge, you can now understand the bigger picture and walk more and more in the light of God's Word. This is how you become a partaker of His grace and peace.

You can't walk in something you don't know or see.

Once you know and understand it has been given to you, you must expand it. We talked about covenant and how our covenant gives us the same rights Jesus received from the Father. Jesus was executed on the cross for us so those rights belong to us, but we have to know them in order to walk in them.

Grace and peace are multiplied to us through the knowledge of the Word of God and the knowledge of our Lord, Jesus Christ. Knowing more about what He did will let us grow in His grace and peace. Do you want more peace in your life? Well, it comes through further knowledge and understanding. It's not just head knowledge—it's revelation knowledge.

We actually change and grow by knowing who we are in Christ and what belongs to us in Him. Picture yourself in a completely dark room with no knowledge of what is in the room with you. Yet, everything you need is in that room. Only when the lights turn on can you see what you need. Once you see them, you can move to them and partake. It is the same with prayer and forgiveness. And it is the same process with all circumstances of life. Depression, jealousy, financial lack or whatever it might be, the Bible lays out for us true doctrine. This way, the light can turn on and we can see where God stands on every issue we're facing in life.

Questions and Prayer:

Are you walking in the grace and peace God has already provided for you? How can you partake in more? Pray today that God would turn on the lights in the room so you can see everything He has given you.

AN AWAKENING

Read: Romans 10:8-11

In today's modern Church, Romans 10:8-11 has come to be known as the prayer of salvation. A lot of people use this prayer to lead others to salvation. Notice that you have to believe with your heart and inner spirit to gain the revelation that God has raised Jesus Christ from the dead.

In these verses, we see "mouth" and "heart" three times. The confession of truth or the revelation that Jesus is Lord comes through revelation knowledge because there has to be an awakening in your spirit. There has to be something that awakens your spirit to confess that Jesus is real, whether the awakening comes as a miracle, during a worship service, or from God speaking to you.

Faith for salvation and salvation itself are not just within a single prayer. The context of verses 8-11 explains that it is a lifelong confession. It is the belief and revelation we receive every day that Jesus Christ is Lord. Salvation is not a single prayer spoken once in a restaurant parking lot and then believing we are saved forever. Neither is it a single event in a Church service where God awakens us and we go to the altar to pray. There is a conception and a reality that takes place in our hearts that shows us God and Jesus are real.

Yes, there is an awakening event. But from there we go out into the world and must act on what we just received. The conception and awakening is only a piece of the process. It is like a wedding. In a marriage, the ceremony is the event, but after the event something else has to take place. The relationship must continue after the ceremony or the marriage will fail.

We have to keep filling our hearts with the Word of God and keep receiving revelation in the Word of God. Then it can bubble forth as you confess what is entrenched in you that Jesus is the Lord!

Confess Today:

Jesus Christ died for me and He is my Savior. He paid for my sins, my iniquities and my transgressions. They were all put upon Him and I believe in Him. Therefore, I confess Jesus Christ as my Lord and Savior. I submit to you Lord, and to the lifelong process of salvation!

FAITH IS ACTION

FAITH IS ACTION

Matthew 14:22-31

²² IMMEDIATELY JESUS MADE HIS DISCIPLES GET INTO THE BOAT AND GO BEFORE HIM TO THE OTHER SIDE, WHILE HE SENT THE MULTITUDES AWAY. ²³ AND WHEN HE HAD SENT THE MULTITUDES AWAY, HE WENT UP ON THE MOUNTAIN BY HIMSELF TO PRAY. NOW WHEN EVENING CAME, HE WAS ALONE THERE. ²⁴ BUT THE BOAT WAS NOW IN THE MIDDLE OF THE SEA, TOSSED BY THE WAVES, FOR THE WIND WAS CONTRARY. ²⁵ NOW IN THE FOURTH WATCH OF THE NIGHT JESUS WENT TO THEM, WALKING ON THE SEA. ²⁶ AND WHEN THE DISCIPLES SAW HIM WALKING ON THE SEA, THEY WERE TROUBLED, SAYING, "IT IS A GHOST!" AND THEY CRIED OUT FOR FEAR. ²⁷ BUT IMMEDIATELY JESUS SPOKE TO THEM, SAYING, "BE OF GOOD CHEER! IT IS I; DO NOT BE AFRAID." ²⁸ AND PETER ANSWERED HIM AND SAID, "LORD, IF IT IS YOU, COMMAND ME TO COME TO YOU ON THE WATER." ²⁹ SO HE SAID, "COME." AND WHEN PETER HAD COME DOWN OUT OF THE BOAT, HE WALKED ON THE WATER TO GO TO JESUS. ³⁰ BUT WHEN HE SAW THAT THE WIND WAS BOISTEROUS, HE WAS AFRAID; AND BEGINNING TO SINK HE CRIED OUT, SAYING, "LORD, SAVE ME!" ³¹ AND IMMEDIATELY JESUS STRETCHED OUT HIS HAND AND CAUGHT HIM, AND SAID TO HIM, "O YOU OF LITTLE FAITH, WHY DID YOU DOUBT?"

1. Faith is a _____ substance and it is not _____ to our five senses. We can't see, feel, or touch our faith, but by faith we believe.

2. God as Creator has _____ over His creation. His Word came first and His authority _____ over all things in the universe.

3. As Christians, our Biblical faith _____ that God is the authority in our lives. So we walk by _____ in Him and in His Word even though our five senses are in _____.

4.   If our faith is not _____ and active then it has no _____, because our faith must have corresponding actions.

5.   The _____ believes that God exists, however, he has no _____ that God is the authority over His creation.

6.   Mankind can be _____ to think and believe in their minds that they are in _____ _____ with God, but if they don't act by doing and hearing God's Word, they have no faith.

7.   When we take our focus off Jesus and place our attention on our _____, our faith leaves and _____ rushes in.

8.   Faith is a spiritual principle much like the law of _____ is in our physical environment and the law of faith _____ for those who walk in it.

9.   It is not natural for us to _____ faith because we have to _____ how to understand faith.

10. When we lose our faith, we are no longer _____ and we are reduced to our own strength.

11. God has preeminence and authority over _____ He created, and this includes the _____ spiritual realm.

12. You are not _____ by works. If your faith has no works, then there is no _____ in your faith.

13. If you _____ Jesus Christ as your Lord and Savior and you believe it in your _____, then you are going to prove it with your actions.

Key Words:

(a) Prophecy   (b) Miracle   (c) Tangible   (d) Relationship   (e) Action

_____ Fellowship with God and involving Him in everything.

_____ Moving and demonstrating faith in God's Word.

_____ Supernatural event held to be an act of God.

_____ Inspired message viewed as revelation from God.

_____ Objects possible to touch, understand or realize.

Session Answers:

1. spiritual, tangible

2. authority, rules

3. believes, faith, opposition

4. alive, value

5. devil, faith

6. deceived, right standing

7. circumstances, fear

8. gravity, works

9. understand, learn

10. supernatural

11. everything, unseen

12. saved, salvation

13. confess, heart

Key Word Answers:

d, e, b, a, c,

STEP OUT IN FAITH

Read: Matthew 14:22-31

I love this story! Stop for a minute and picture the scene in your mind. The disciples are in a boat in the middle of a terrible storm. They look over the side and see Jesus in the middle of the sea walking on the water. Suddenly, Peter shouts out to Him:

"If You are willing, I will come."

Peter gets out of the boat and begins to walk on the water. Peter is doing the supernatural. And in Verse 24 we are told, "The boat was now in the middle of the sea, tossed by the waves, for the wind was contrary." This was the condition of the storm before Peter stepped out of the boat. However, only when Peter took his attention and focus off of Jesus and looked at the circumstances around him did his faith leave and doubt filled him.

You have to ask, what kept Peter above the water? The Word of God and Peter's faith is what kept him walking on the water. He had received the Word of Jesus to come to Him. This told Peter that if he wanted to walk on the water, all he had to do was go to Jesus. It was God, through Jesus, that ordained Peter to walk on the water.

Peter stepped out of the boat and began to walk on the water only as long as his eyes were fixed on Jesus. That was how he was able to do the supernatural. When he took his eyes off Jesus, his faith left and fear entered him, so he began to sink. God didn't push him down or dunk him under the water. It was his faith leaving him and fear coming in that made Peter sink.

Questions and Prayer:

When have you recently stepped out in faith? How can you keep your eyes on Jesus and not fall into doubt? Pray today that God would give you boldness and courage to step out more often in faith.

FAITH IS UNSEEN

Read: Hebrews 11:1-3

Hebrews 11 is dedicated to the subject of faith. Faith has to be acted upon because it is not faith unless it is acted upon. Faith is not tangible; it is hoped for in the future but not seen. Faith is also not tangible to our five natural senses, but we believe it is there.

In Verses 1 and 3 we read, "Now faith is the substance of things hoped for, the evidence of things not seen…By faith we believe the worlds were framed by the Word of God…" His Word came before anything else was brought into existence. God's Word was first, and His Word framed the world. He spoke it and it came into existence, which means His Word has authority over everything our five senses engage with.

Let's go back to the Garden and ask, why did Adam fall? Picture Satan telling him that he shall not surely die, meaning, Adam doesn't have to fear God. Satan told Adam he did not have to worry about disobeying God or about having any consequences to his evil actions. The second lie Satan told Adam was that he would be as a god and determine good and evil for himself. Satan was telling Adam he could go above his Creator and would not have to worry about God's authority over His creation to judge.

What we see here is that faith brings us back to the beginning and truth that God is the Creator of all things. God and His Word have authority over everything we can see, touch, feel, smell or hear with our senses. Taking it a step further, we can include the unseen realm as well, because God and His Word have preeminence and authority over everything. As believers, this is the starting point of our faith and where we begin to learn that God is God.

Questions and Prayer:

Ask God to increase your faith and to give you supernatural ability to see the unseen.

PERSONAL DEVOTION SESSION 5 // DAY 3

YOU ARE THE MESSIAH

Read: Hebrews 11:23-29

Moses grew up in Pharaoh's house with Pharaoh's daughter as his mother, yet Moses refused to be called her son. As you read today's Scripture, see how each verse starts with, "By faith," "By faith," "By faith." Please understand faith has to have action! It is not faith if there is no action.

Faith is hearing God's Word speak to us, and because we believe that God is God, we act on His Word. Without trusting God, we go through life doing whatever we want even though we know it is not God's plan. That is exactly what Adam and Judas did.

Peter did the opposite because he knew who Jesus was and he confessed it several times in John 6 and Matthew 14. Peter kept confessing that Jesus was the Lord, the Christ, and the Messiah. Peter's weakness was not due to the fact that he never put Jesus in the position of Creator. His weakness was in his own flesh, within himself.

Likewise in Hebrews 11, we learn that the actions of Abel, Abraham and Moses reveal faith is more than belief. We must demonstrate our faith daily through our actions, thoughts and words. Church attendance is not enough. Our actions serve as evidence of our faith.

On the other hand, Judas thought he was smarter than Jesus and he felt he had a better plan. What was he doing? Judas was putting himself above Jesus. Whenever mankind puts themselves above God, they're in trouble. Saints, just think about how lost we are in the first place.

The Bible tells us it is not in man to know how to direct his own steps. This means that it is not in man to direct his steps toward God.

What then is faith? Faith believes that God is God and that He is the authority over our lives. It is believing in what He says and acting upon His Word.

Questions and Prayer:

Have you surrendered your will to God's will? How? What can you do to surrender your will to His? Pray today that your steps wouldn't be led by your own desires, but by God's desires.

FAITH IS ALIVE

Read: James 2

We are asked two questions in James 2. What does it profit my brethren if someone says they have faith, and they have no actions to their faith? And can his faith save him? The Bible says, no. The Bible tells us that if you do not act on your faith, you have no faith.

We read that if faith has no works then it is dead. It is meaningless, fruitless. What do the demons believe? They believe that God is God, but they do not put Him in the position of authority as Creator. Works and faith must go together.

You are not saved by works. And if your faith has no works, then there is no salvation in your faith. Even Abraham was told to do something, and it was his acting on that Word that caused him to receive righteousness and have it accounted to him.

So if you say that you have faith and confess Jesus Christ as Lord and Savior, yet you don't act on what Jesus tells you to do, what good is what you say? That is what these verses of Scripture are telling us. Faith without works is dead. Faith has to be combined with action.

How then are we saved by faith? We are saved through faith, and not just by thinking it, but acting on it! Every single promise of God and what He has given us comes by revelation knowledge, a belief in our hearts, and by acting on it. If you know it but don't act on it, you don't have faith in it. You have to understand that God is looking for active faith in you!

Questions and Prayer:

Is your faith active? What do you believe in? Write down five things that can activate your faith. Pray that God will give you an increased measure of faith to believe in.

DOES JESUS KNOW YOU?

Read: Matthew 7

When I first came into Christianity, this passage from Matthew scared me. Here we learn of people who thought their whole lives that they had a relationship with Jesus Christ, but they did not! They said to the Lord, didn't we prophesize in your name, didn't we do many wonders in Your name, and didn't we work for You? Yet it was too late for them.

The Bible warns that many will say in that day, "Lord, Lord," yet God will say to them that He doesn't even know them. He will tell them that He never had a relationship with them. How does this happen?

Well, when you lean back from the story and look at what He is saying, it's quite obvious. Listen, when you come face-to-face with Jesus Christ are you going to tell Him how great you are? Are you going to say, "Hey, didn't I do these things in Your name?" I don't think so! I know I will be saying, "Thank You for everything I have and all You have done for me!"

The people in this chapter of Matthew never put Jesus in the position of their Lord and Savior. This is the key difference between your head and your heart. In their heads, they thought they were strong with God. I am sure when Judas went out with them, two by two, and miracles happened, he probably thought he was good too!

You have to be sure of this! Many people will live their entire lives filling out forms in Church claiming to be Christians! They will know all the right answers in Church, and some will even serve in Church. They will think they had a right relationship with the Lord, but they didn't!

In Verse 26, there are those who hear the Word of God but don't act upon what they hear. Their faith is not active, and they will be likened unto a foolish man. In the end, it all comes down to hearing and doing the Word of God.

If you confess Jesus Christ as your Lord and Savior and you believe it in your heart, then you are going to prove it with your actions. You are going to be active and walk in your belief because you know what He did for you. If you say, "Yes, I believe in Jesus Christ," but you go out and do whatever you want while never engaging with His Word, then it won't matter whether you attend Church or not. Think about it—even Judas went to Church!

Questions and Prayer:

Is your salvation active or passive? How can you ensure you don't end up like the people in Matthew 7? Today, pray that God would give you a desire to be active in your salvation and a desire to know Him more.

SALVATION IS A RELATIONSHIP

SESSION 6
SALVATION IS A RELATIONSHIP

Luke 22:54-62

[54] HAVING ARRESTED HIM, THEY LED HIM AND BROUGHT HIM INTO THE HIGH PRIEST'S HOUSE. BUT PETER FOLLOWED AT A DISTANCE. [55] NOW WHEN THEY HAD KINDLED A FIRE IN THE MIDST OF THE COURTYARD AND SAT DOWN TOGETHER, PETER SAT AMONG THEM. [56] AND A CERTAIN SERVANT GIRL, SEEING HIM AS HE SAT BY THE FIRE, LOOKED INTENTLY AT HIM AND SAID, "THIS MAN WAS ALSO WITH HIM." [57] BUT HE DENIED HIM, SAYING, "WOMAN, I DO NOT KNOW HIM." [58] AND AFTER A LITTLE WHILE ANOTHER SAW HIM AND SAID, "YOU ALSO ARE OF THEM." BUT PETER SAID, "MAN, I AM NOT!" [59] THEN AFTER ABOUT AN HOUR HAD PASSED, ANOTHER CONFIDENTLY AFFIRMED, SAYING, "SURELY THIS FELLOW ALSO WAS WITH HIM, FOR HE IS A GALILEAN." [60] BUT PETER SAID, "MAN, I DO NOT KNOW WHAT YOU ARE SAYING!" IMMEDIATELY, WHILE HE WAS STILL SPEAKING, THE ROOSTER CROWED. [61] AND THE LORD TURNED AND LOOKED AT PETER. AND PETER REMEMBERED THE WORD OF THE LORD, HOW HE HAD SAID TO HIM, "BEFORE THE ROOSTER CROWS, YOU WILL DENY ME THREE TIMES." [62] SO PETER WENT OUT AND WEPT BITTERLY.

1. Salvation brings a _____-_____ Spirit, which is alive to God, and this experience is the _____ _____ of our human spirit.

2. To be _____ of the Spirit is to have a relationship with God again. Our hearts are now _____ to God because we believe He is the Creator and the _____ over His creation.

3. We must be alive to God and produce _____ or _____ based on the Word of God, and the only way we can produce fruit is through Jesus.

4. We are to _____ in Christ and live for Him every day. God wants our fruit to show the world that we believe in _____ and His Word.

5. Salvation can be _____ through _____ and living without regard to God any longer.

6. Salvation is not an _____ but a relationship. Similar to a wedding being the event, but the _____ is the relationship.

7. Either God is God and you _____ in Him as Your _____ or He is not. We have to be all-in for Jesus because He was _____-_____ for us.

8. The seed is planted in your _____ but the fruit is the action of the Word. Actions are an _____ sign of your _____ belief.

9. When you experience the new birth you move from _____ and condemnation over to _____ and righteousness.

10. If you leave the question of salvation up to assumption and _____, then there is a huge possibility of _____ in your decision.

11. We must look to the _____ for revelation knowledge in order to _____ if we have salvation or not.

12. Our salvation is _____ once we are dead.

13. Adam died _____ because he was disconnected from God. He died _____ because sin entered him and he became depressed and felt fear, shame and guilt. Then the Bible tells us that eventually Adam died _____.

14. Every branch that is _____ _____ must bear fruit and do the work of God. Every branch that is not doing this will be _____ _____.

15. The world and all of humanity is _____ before God and His _____ of judgment is on all of us.

Key Words:

(a) Confession of Faith   (b) Condemned   (c) Zealot   (d) Fruit   (e) Abide

_____ Gain deliverance from a life of sin through service to God.

_____ Heavenly verdict signifying punishment and damnation.

_____ To remain and stay spiritually connected with Christ.

_____ Section of the Pharisees who were antagonistic to the Romans.

_____ Admitting and acknowledging the truth that Jesus is Lord.

Session Answers:

1. born-again, new birth

2. born, alive, authority

3. fruit, actions

4. abide, Jesus

5. lost, unbelief

6. event, marriage

7. trust, Savior, all-in

8. heart, outward, inner

9. guilt, justification

10. speculation, error

11. Bible, know

12. sealed

13. spiritually, soulishly, physically

14. in Christ, cut away

15. condemned, wrath

Key Word Answers:

d, b, e, c, a

FUNDAMENTAL DIFFERENCE

Read: Luke 22:47-53

Two disciples make up the story in Luke 22. Judas is prideful and arrogant and thinks he is more intelligent than Jesus and has a better plan. Many scholars believe that Judas formulated his plan to turn Jesus over for thirty pieces of silver in the belief that this would force Jesus to side with the zealots of the time. There is a lot of different commentary on this event, but we are not going to know the whole truth until we get to heaven.

We also see Peter during the same 24-hour period. Peter knows that the Lord told him he would deny Him three times. And as we know, Peter fulfilled this prophecy. The crucial difference between Judas and Peter is that Peter wept bitterly over his denial of Jesus.

These two men walked together and lived out their weaknesses, but there was something very different inside of them. One went on to honor, while the other went on to shame.

Remember when Jesus told His disciples at the Last Supper that one of them was going to betray Him? And remember how no one could pick Judas out of the crowd? They could not pick him out of a line-up or say he was the one because he acted like a believer. He looked like he fit in with the rest of the twelve.

To be honest, I would have voted for Peter, because Jesus had already attributed Satan's influence to him and he was always getting into trouble. Peter was sinking in the sea and he was told he had little faith. When you look at the two, Peter did have a lot of incorrect answers and actions—but there was something fundamentally different inside these two apostles. The fundamental difference was active faith. Peter had active faith, Judas did not.

Questions and Prayer:

Who would you have picked to betray and deny Jesus at the Last Supper? How can we be sure we won't fall into the same category as Judas? Pray today that you would draw near to the Lord as He would draw near to you.

CONFESSION OF FAITH

Read: John 3

In this passage, we learn quite a bit about salvation. In fact, this is the only time in Scripture that the phrase "born-again" is used. We learn that Nicodemus has a curious heart that recognizes Jesus is not a phony because He is from God. This is a confession of faith from Nicodemus about Jesus.

Then Jesus throws a curveball in Verse 5: unless a man is born-again, he cannot see the kingdom of God. Jesus explains in Verse 6, "That which is born of the flesh is flesh, and that which is born of the Spirit is spirit." In other words, the born-again experience is a new birth of our human spirit. It is coming alive to God.

In Verse 18, Jesus explains the earth is broken up into two groups. All of humanity is born in condemnation and guilt and separated from God. We are born unrighteous and destined for an eternity in hell, meaning, separation from God. This is a difficult thing for humanity to get their arms around, but it's the truth. This is why each of us must look to the Bible for revelation knowledge to learn what is right. We cannot formulate the truth in our minds.

God is basically saying those who don't believe in Jesus are already condemned. This means that those who are ignorant of who God is or what God's plan and purpose is are condemned already. But those who believe in Him are not condemned.

Questions and Prayer:

Have you been born-again? Do you understand what it means to be born-again? Today, pray that the Lord would reveal to you what it means to be born-again and to come alive by His Spirit.

JESUS BRINGS LIFE

Read: John 15

What did we learn about covenant language? We learned that "in Him," "with Him," "by Him" and "through Him" are covenant terms, meaning, every branch in Him is a branch connected to Him because He is the Vine.

Picture a vine with many branches. Jesus is that vine, and He brings the life source to all the branches. God is the vine-dresser, the husbandman or gardener, who prunes the branches that are you and me.

Jesus says that every branch in Me bears fruit—or takes action and lives the Word of God. The Word of God is the seed planted in your heart, but the fruit is your action based on the Word. We are told, "But the fruit of the Spirit is love, joy, peace, longsuffering, kindness, goodness, faithfulness, gentleness, self-control" (Galatians 5:22). All of these are actions. They are outward fruit based upon the Word we have in our hearts. Jesus said every branch that is in Me and acts on the revealed Word will be fruitful in life. Every branch in Me that is not acting on My Word will be cut away.

I want you to know Jesus is saying He is the life source, and if you are in Me and engaged in Me, you have to be fruitful. If you love Me, you have to be doing My Word.

Questions and Prayer:

What kind of fruit are you bearing? Do your actions line up with the "Fruit of the Spirit?" Pray that God would make you fruitful and your faith pure.

BEARING FRUIT

Read: Luke 8:9-19

This is a common parable about the sower and the seed. We learn the seed is the Word of God and the ones who are by the wayside are the people who hear the Word. The first person heard the Word, but Satan took it away before the Word could become fruitful in their life. The second person was in a stony and rocky place, and believed in the Word for a little while but then fell away and becomes unfruitful, or having no salvation. The third person heard the Word and grew, but while growing, they became unfruitful. In other words, they were bearing fruit but the cares and riches of this world choked the Word out of them, making them unfruitful. Then they fell away. The fourth person, however, heard the Word and grew in the Word and continued to bear fruit, some thirty, sixty or a hundred-fold.

This process is not something done in a short period of time. No, it's a process that continues throughout your life. You keep hearing the Word and receiving revelation, and then, by faith in the Word, you act on the Word.

What is the result of this process? The result is that you keep bearing fruit all your life!

What happens to the others by the wayside and in stony, rocky places? Sadly, they fall away and are cut off because the Word meant nothing to them.

Salvation is not an event but a lifelong relationship between you and Jesus as your Creator, King, Master and Savior. Salvation is based on knowledge, not ignorance. Salvation is based on knowing Who Jesus is, growing into His image, and doing what He taught us in His Word. We are transformed back from the image of Adam and into the image of Jesus.

Questions and Prayer:

Is the seed in your heart planted in rich soil or has it fallen by the wayside? Are you continuing to grow in the Word and bearing fruit every day? What do you think your fruit looks like in God's eyes?

NO DEBATE

Read: Romans 11:13-22

We don't gain salvation through works; We receive salvation by faith. So how do we leave our salvation behind? We leave salvation through unbelief. These verses in Romans 11 are very sobering on this subject.

Because Christ died for us, we have an obligation to live for Him. We have an obligation to live our entire lives for Him because He gave His life for us. It's not a debate! Either you love Him and you position Him as Lord, Savior and King of your life, or you don't. The choice is yours!

If Jesus lives in your heart, then He wants you to answer His call—not yours. We forsake our path for His path. Sobering, isn't it? The Book of Ephesians tells us not to partake in the sins of the world, otherwise you will partake in the world's damnation.

When people tell me they believe in the "once saved, always saved" approach, I ask them why they believe that Jesus has no expectation on them as a Christian.

Consider two people who marry, come together, and stay together of their own free will. If one of them departs for a long dispensation of time, what happens to the marriage relationship? Salvation is a covenant relationship where we bind ourselves to Jesus and to God. We do this with an oath of our very lives, which is our reasonable services because of what Jesus and God did for us through the covenant.

Questions and Prayer:

What is the most sobering part of this message? Why should you submit your will to His will? Pray today that the Lord would give you strength to follow and submit to His will and plan.

SESSION 7

DEALING WITH THE PENALTY OF SIN

DEALING WITH THE PENALTY OF SIN

John 20:12-23

¹² AND SHE SAW TWO ANGELS IN WHITE SITTING, ONE AT THE HEAD AND THE OTHER AT THE FEET, WHERE THE BODY OF JESUS HAD LAIN. ¹³ THEN THEY SAID TO HER, "WOMAN, WHY ARE YOU WEEPING?" SHE SAID TO THEM, "BECAUSE THEY HAVE TAKEN AWAY MY LORD, AND I DO NOT KNOW WHERE THEY HAVE LAID HIM." ¹⁴ NOW WHEN SHE HAD SAID THIS, SHE TURNED AROUND AND SAW JESUS STANDING THERE, AND DID NOT KNOW THAT IT WAS JESUS. ¹⁵ JESUS SAID TO HER, "WOMAN, WHY ARE YOU WEEPING? WHOM ARE YOU SEEKING?" SHE, SUPPOSING HIM TO BE THE GARDENER, SAID TO HIM, "SIR, IF YOU HAVE CARRIED HIM AWAY, TELL ME WHERE YOU HAVE LAID HIM, AND I WILL TAKE HIM AWAY." ¹⁶ JESUS SAID TO HER, "MARY!" SHE TURNED AND SAID TO HIM, "RABBONI!" (WHICH IS TO SAY, TEACHER). ¹⁷ JESUS SAID TO HER, "DO NOT CLING TO ME, FOR I HAVE NOT YET ASCENDED TO MY FATHER; BUT GO TO MY BRETHREN AND SAY TO THEM, 'I AM ASCENDING TO MY FATHER AND YOUR FATHER, AND TO MY GOD AND YOUR GOD.'" ¹⁸ MARY MAGDALENE CAME AND TOLD THE DISCIPLES THAT SHE HAD SEEN THE LORD, AND THAT HE HAD SPOKEN THESE THINGS TO HER. ¹⁹ THEN, THE SAME DAY AT EVENING, BEING THE FIRST DAY OF THE WEEK, WHEN THE DOORS WERE SHUT WHERE THE DISCIPLES WERE ASSEMBLED, FOR FEAR OF THE JEWS, JESUS CAME AND STOOD IN THE MIDST, AND SAID TO THEM, "PEACE BE WITH YOU." ²⁰ WHEN HE HAD SAID THIS, HE SHOWED THEM HIS HANDS AND HIS SIDE. THEN THE DISCIPLES WERE GLAD WHEN THEY SAW THE LORD. ²¹ SO JESUS SAID TO THEM AGAIN, "PEACE TO YOU! AS THE FATHER HAS SENT ME, I ALSO SEND YOU." ²² AND WHEN HE HAD SAID THIS, HE BREATHED ON THEM, AND SAID TO THEM, "RECEIVE THE HOLY SPIRIT. ²³ IF YOU FORGIVE THE SINS OF ANY, THEY ARE FORGIVEN THEM; IF YOU RETAIN THE SINS OF ANY, THEY ARE RETAINED."

1. When Jesus died on the cross, His soul and Spirit were separated from His _____. He went into the belly of the earth and He _____ to the _____ in hell.

2. Hell had two compartments before the _____. One was a Place of _____ and the other was called Paradise or Abraham's Bosom.

3. The Old Testament Saints went to a place called _____ because they were still _____ dead, but _____ was accounted to them since they had faith in the coming Messiah.

4. After His resurrection, Jesus was seen by Mary at the tomb, and He told her not to touch Him because He still had things to _____.

5. When Jesus died on the cross His soul and Spirit were _____ from His body. His body was buried in the tomb, but His soul and Spirit did not _____ to exist.

6. You may die _____ on earth but you do not cease to exist. Everyone will spend eternity somewhere. It will be either in _____ or in _____. When a born-again Christian dies today they go straight to heaven.

7. After the resurrection, Jesus sent the disciples out two-by-two, but first He _____ on them and it was the breath of the _____ _____. They were now alive to God.

8. We must do more than believe God _____. We must believe that He is our Lord and Savior and that an awful price was paid on our _____.

9. Showing remorse or regret or sorrow for your _____ does not gain you salvation because salvation only comes through _____.

10. Once you are in a relationship with Christ it is _____ to lose your salvation if you continue to _____ Him.

Key Words:

(a) Sin   (b) Atonement   (c) Remorse   (d) High Priest   (e) Repent

_____ It was his duty to represent the whole people; a Levitical order of respect.

_____ Reconciliation between God and man through Jesus Christ; covering over of sin.

_____ Disobedience to the laws of God; lawlessness.

_____ Distress from a sense of guilt for past wrongs.

_____ Involving a change for the better and turning back to God.

Session Answers:

1. body, preached, spirits

2. resurrection, Torment

3. Paradise, spiritually, righteousness

4. accomplish

5. separated, cease

6. physically, heaven, hell

7. breathed, new birth

8. exists, behalf

9. sins, faith

10. difficult, pursue

Key Word Answers:

d, b, a, c, e

THIRTY PIECES OF SILVER

Read: Matthew 27:1-10

Throughout this series we have explored the motives of two apostles, Peter and Judas. Today, I want to focus on Judas during the night of his betrayal. He was paid thirty pieces of silver to bring soldiers to a place of isolation where Jesus was. A place where there would not be multitudes of people. Judas was paid for the opportunity to seize Jesus without a crowd nearby. The Jewish leaders did not want to start a riot or cause any violence. Understand that Judas had no idea they were going to condemn and crucify Jesus.

In fact, in the Gospel of Mark when the soldiers came to arrest Jesus, Judas kissed Him and told the soldiers to bind Him and lead Him away safely. In other words, Judas asked that Jesus be kept safe. If Judas knew Jesus was going to be executed, that would have been the perfect place and opportune time because there was no crowd. But Judas had no idea the arrest of Jesus was going to turn into a public spectacle and Jesus would be falsely accused.

When Judas learned of Jesus' fate, the Bible tells us he had great remorse and regretted his actions. Judas even went back to the high priests, threw the money down, and told them he didn't want the money. He did not realize what he had done, and he told the high priest he had sinned against innocent blood. There was great remorse in Judas. Yet, fundamentally, nothing inside his heart had changed.

We must understand we can say we are sorry and be remorseful for our sins, but our salvation does not come through our actions. Salvation comes through our faith in Jesus Christ. Then, faith is followed by our actions. Judas never made that jump. We will study this more later, but for now, I want you to understand the heart of Judas even though he tried to undo things and make them right. When his efforts failed, Judas did not repent; he hung himself instead.

Questions and Prayer:

What mistake did Judas make? How can we be certain we won't fall into the trap of unbelief in our hearts? Pray today that you will receive faith and forgiveness in areas where you are lacking.

THE ULTIMATE VICTORY

Read: 1 Peter 3

In this passage of Scripture, we learn Jesus went into the belly of the earth and preached. "For as Jonah was three days and three nights in the belly of the great fish, so will the Son of Man be three days and three nights in the heart of the earth" (Matthew 12:40). So Jesus went into the earth and preached, but He did not preach about salvation, He proclaims!

During those three days, Jesus' soul and Spirit were separated from His body. His body was buried and laid in a tomb, but His soul and Spirit continued just like every other Saint who had died before Him. You see, Jesus did not cease to exist like some people believe happens when we die. In Luke 16, we learned that no one ever ceases to exist.

Even though we die physically and have a funeral here on earth, we still live on eternally. We will study this further as we go along in this series, but Jesus went into the belly of the earth for three days and three nights. He preached, He proclaimed, and He met with and saw other Saints who were there. Jesus called out a specific group of people who had lived during the time of Noah and He preached to them.

During those three days, Jesus conquered death, hell and the grave. He gained the ultimate victory so we can each spend eternity with Him.

You have to believe in your heart that Jesus did all these things. Jesus died. He won the battle. Then He rose from the dead. These are the requirements for your salvation.

Questions and Prayer:

What is the message of salvation? Have you shared it with anyone recently? Pray today that you will have the courage to share Jesus with someone you know. Let your life be the light leading others to salvation.

JESUS BREATHED ON THEM

Read: John 20

A lot happens in this chapter of John, and I want you to notice Verse 19 because these events all happen in one day on the first day of the week, a Sunday.

The first thing Jesus did when He came back to see His disciples was breathe on them. This was the breath of the new birth. Then on the Day of Pentecost, they went out.

Do you remember the last time God breathed on someone? The last time this happened was with Adam when he became a living soul. When Jesus breathed on His disciples, they became living spirits. They became alive to God. At that moment the Spirit of God came into them.

The only way the Spirit of God could come into them was if they were righteous enough to receive the Spirit of God.

Because of unrighteousness and spiritual separation from God, even Abraham in death could not go into the presence of God. Abraham's righteousness was only "accounted to him." It was the same for David—his righteousness was also accounted to him.

But after Jesus' resurrection, everything changed!

We are made righteous! The Spirit of God now lives in us. Jesus accomplished this plan for us. Praise God!

Questions and Prayer:

What is righteousness? How are you made righteous? Ask God today to breathe on you. Ask God for His Spirit to come into you.

ALL THINGS RECONCILED

Read: 2 Corinthians 5

In Verses 17-19, Paul tells us that if anyone is in covenant with the Lord, Jesus Christ, or if anyone believes in Him as their Lord and Savior with active living faith, then they are a new creation. In other words, we are a complete new order of creation, or an entirely new level of creation. God formed this new creation of born-again, Spirit-filled Christians after the resurrection of Jesus Christ. The Bible tells us old things have passed away and all things have become new. Nothing happened to us physically, only spiritually. We didn't get more hair or lose weight, and even though we have an awakening of Jesus Christ in our soulish realm, we are still battling with the world.

What happened and changed is that spiritually we changed. Spiritually, we have a born-again spirit alive to God. That means our whole relationship with God has changed. This is why Verse 17 says all things have become new. Why? Because Jesus and the Father dealt with the penalty of sin that was imposed upon humanity, and the first piece of that was spiritual death.

We read in Verse 18 that all things were reconciled through God. How did God reconcile all things? Through Jesus Christ. He brought us back to Him. That means our sins are not imputed to us because we are alive to God. My sins and your sins were put upon Jesus Christ. This is why when we sin as Christians, we turn back to the truth and repent. We confess our sins and the blood of Jesus forgives us. We walk in perpetual life because our spirit is alive unto God.

Questions and Prayer:

In what ways are you a new creation? How has Christ transformed your life? Pray today that God would continue to do more inside of you each and every day.

POSITION YOURSELF TO RECEIVE

Read: John 16

Jesus had many more things to tell His disciples, but before the resurrection, they could not understand it. That's because they had no way of understanding the revelation without the Spirit of God inside of them. When the Spirit of God comes into us, things are revealed and come to life in us. They are ignited in our hearts because the Spirit of God is guiding us. We put ourselves in a position to receive revelation knowledge when we go to Church and our pastors give us a Word that is inspired by the Holy Spirit. It's the Holy Spirit who is in us and Jesus who work together to give us revelation. This is so we can act in faith in the revelation knowledge and bear fruit in our lives.

Several times in this chapter, we are told the Holy Spirit will lead and guide us into truth. He will take whatever He sees and hears of the Father and speak it to us. Whatever is given to Jesus, the Holy Spirit will declare it to us. That's the predominant ministry of the Holy Spirit. It is to declare and reveal the things of God to us. Again, we cannot walk in what we don't know, and we cannot live in what we don't understand. We can't embrace any of the promises of God that were given to Jesus and us unless we know them fully in our hearts, activate our faith, and walk in them. This is how important it is to have the Holy Spirit living in us, allowing Him to continually be our tutor, because in the Word He shows us the things of Jesus Christ.

Questions and Prayer:

When have you had a revelation of a spiritual truth? How has that changed you? Pray today that God would open your heart to the revelation knowledge of Christ.

SALVATION OF THE SOUL - POWER OVER SIN

SALVATION OF THE SOUL - POWER OVER SIN

Reading Assignment: Romans 8:1-10

[1] THERE IS THEREFORE NOW NO CONDEMNATION TO THOSE WHO ARE IN CHRIST JESUS, WHO DO NOT WALK ACCORDING TO THE FLESH, BUT ACCORDING TO THE SPIRIT. [2] FOR THE LAW OF THE SPIRIT OF LIFE IN CHRIST JESUS HAS MADE ME FREE FROM THE LAW OF SIN AND DEATH. [3] FOR WHAT THE LAW COULD NOT DO IN THAT IT WAS WEAK THROUGH THE FLESH, GOD DID BY SENDING HIS OWN SON IN THE LIKENESS OF SINFUL FLESH, ON ACCOUNT OF SIN: HE CONDEMNED SIN IN THE FLESH, [4] THAT THE RIGHTEOUS REQUIREMENT OF THE LAW MIGHT BE FULFILLED IN US WHO DO NOT WALK ACCORDING TO THE FLESH BUT ACCORDING TO THE SPIRIT. [5] FOR THOSE WHO LIVE ACCORDING TO THE FLESH SET THEIR MINDS ON THE THINGS OF THE FLESH, BUT THOSE WHO LIVE ACCORDING TO THE SPIRIT, THE THINGS OF THE SPIRIT. [6] FOR TO BE CARNALLY MINDED IS DEATH, BUT TO BE SPIRITUALLY MINDED IS LIFE AND PEACE. [7] BECAUSE THE CARNAL MIND IS ENMITY AGAINST GOD; FOR IT IS NOT SUBJECT TO THE LAW OF GOD, NOR INDEED CAN BE. [8] SO THEN, THOSE WHO ARE IN THE FLESH CANNOT PLEASE GOD. [9] BUT YOU ARE NOT IN THE FLESH BUT IN THE SPIRIT, IF INDEED THE SPIRIT OF GOD DWELLS IN YOU. NOW IF ANYONE DOES NOT HAVE THE SPIRIT OF CHRIST, HE IS NOT HIS. [10] AND IF CHRIST IS IN YOU, THE BODY IS DEAD BECAUSE OF SIN, BUT THE SPIRIT IS LIFE BECAUSE OF RIGHTEOUSNESS.

1. Sin still resides in our _____, and if left unchecked can lead the body to gratification, and our minds will _____.

2. Our mind is saying _____; but our spirit is saying no. We must _____ the tug of war and overcome the internal struggles of everyday life.

3. In the Garden, Jesus was in _____ because His mind wanted another way, but His Spirit _____ the Father.

4. We struggle when we are _____ with opportunities to sin throughout each day. Our spirit is saved and _____ to God but the struggle now is for the _____ of the mind and the soul.

5. We do not walk according to the _____ of the flesh. Instead, we walk according to the Spirit.

6. When we receive revelation knowledge we _____ ourselves and _____ Jesus. Every time we go through this process we _____ a little piece of ourselves.

7. The spirit of our lives in Jesus Christ allows us to overcome the _____ _____ _____ as long as we are being filled with revelation _____ and faith.

8. The _____ of our minds is a lifelong journey to continuously _____, clean and renew our minds.

9. We have a carnal mind and a spiritual mind. The _____ mind is not subject to the _____ of God and the things of God because it is driven by the desires of the flesh or the five senses.

10. God _____ us and renews our minds through trials and tests. It is our _____ in Him during these times of pressure that causes the renewing of our minds.

11. The struggle itself does not change us. It is our _____ in God's _____ that matures and strengthens us. We are not to be _____ by the ways of the world, but rather we are to be _____.

12. The renewing of our minds is _____ Jesus, who saved our spirits, to _____ our minds so that our flesh is put under.

13. Don't conform to the world and don't be _____ by the world. The world is driven by fallen man and _____ is their guide.

Key Words:

(a) Law   (b) Carnal   (c) Agape Love   (d) Conform   (e) Phileo Love

_____ Selfless, sacrificial, unconditional love; the kind of love Jesus has for the Father.

_____ Governed by mere human nature, not by the Spirit of God.

_____ Brotherly love for fellow humans; care, respect and compassion for each other.

_____ Revealed will of God given to restrain the evil tendencies of fallen man.

_____ Having the same form as another, rendering to the image of God's Son.

Sessions Answers:

1. flesh, struggle
2. yes, win
3. agony, obeyed
4. confronted, alive, salvation
5. desires
6. humble, exalt, forsake
7. law of sin, knowledge
8. renewing, sanctify
9. carnal, laws
10. matures, trusting
11. faith, promises, conformed, transformed
12. allowing, control
13. molded, Satan

Key Word Answers:

c, b, e, a, d

THE STRUGGLE IS REAL

Read: Luke 22:39-45

In the Garden before His crucifixion, Jesus was in agony in His mind. Remember, He was walking into a crucifixion that He agreed to accept. After all, He was God and wrote the prophecies. He wrote Psalm 22 where we learn about His roaring and His bones out of joint. He wrote that they wagged their heads at Me and they will put Me to shame with a crown of thorns on My head. They will falsely accuse Me.

Confronted with this, Jesus asked, "Father if there was any other way to accomplish this, let it happen, but nevertheless let Your will be done. Father, I will do Your will."

This is a minor comparison, but we have the same struggles in our lives. Every day we are confronted with opportunities to sin. We are confronted with our body, the world system, Satan, our friends, family, and the news media. They are all telling us to do something that is not God's will—things that are not in line with God's Word and are not God's best for us. Furthermore, we know it is not of God. Therefore, we have a choice, and our decision is determined in our minds.

Though our spirits are saved and alive to God, our minds can still rob us of complete happiness. One negative word from somebody we love can cause us to fall into depression. After salvation, the daily struggle is no longer a struggle for eternal life, but is a struggle for salvation of the mind and soul.

Questions and Prayer:

What are the things you battle with in your mind every day? How can you begin to renew your mind unto salvation? Today, pray that God would renew your mind and give you the mind of Christ.

THE DECISION IS YOURS

Read: Romans 8

I love this chapter because it begins with these words: "There is therefore now no condemnation to those who are in Christ Jesus…" But don't stop there because the verse continues with, "…who do not walk according to the flesh…" This refers to the desires of the flesh. Instead, we as Christians "…walk according to the Spirit."

There are two sides pulling and prodding each of us. Remember the cartoon with the good guy on one shoulder and the bad guy on the other? One is whispering for you to go one way and the other is whispering for you to go the other way. This always leaves you with a decision to make. What is your answer?

This process happens every day, but we are guided by the Spirit of life we have in Jesus Christ to make the right decisions. This frees us from the law of sin in our lives. The best example I can give you is of an airplane and the law of gravity. An airplane weighs thousands of pounds, and gravity would surely bring that plane to the ground if it weren't for the aerodynamic law of thrust and lift. When a plane speeds down the runway and gains enough thrust and lift so it can overcome the law of gravity. This is the same concept of force we have as Christians. The Spirit of Jesus Christ lives in us and allows us to overcome the law of sin and condemnation, as long as that life is being filled with revelation and produces faith in action.

The carnal mind is not subject to the laws and things of God, but our renewed spiritual mind is. In our mind, we either listen to the world, Satan, and our own lustful desires or we listen to the Word of God and His plan and purpose. You must train your mind according to the Word of God.

Questions and Prayer:

Do you ever face condemnation, guilt or shame? What do you do when that happens? Ask God to take away the condemnation and fill you with thoughts of confidence.

YOUR ACTIONS GLORIFY GOD

Read: 1 Peter 1:4-5

Again, when it comes to salvation, it's a cooperative effort. We must have faith and God must act, but think about it—God already acted! God gave us the grace of Jesus Christ, and it's our decision to exercise our faith. If we make the decision and activate our faith, we engage in salvation. God's power sustains us as long as our faith is engaged with Him in a meaningful relationship. Remember, salvation is not a single event that happens at the awakening. Salvation starts at this event, but it continues with your lifelong journey. Our salvation is sealed at our physical deaths, but it is completed at the resurrection when our bodies are saved.

In 1 Peter 4:6-9, Peter tells us we are kept by the power of God through our faith, even though we go through trials and tests in life. Satan will come at you. The world will come at you. Your friends will come at you. Situations will arise where you will have to make decisions that are very uncomfortable to your flesh. But when you activate your faith in God's Word to come against that difficult situation, you will be glorifying God with your actions. No one enjoys these trials and tests, but you glorify God when you side with His Word.

For example, changing friends or unhealthy patterns from your past is all part of the struggle, because what was right now becomes wrong. What you accepted then you no longer accept now. This causes internal turmoil, but the Bible tells us that when you are tested and your faith is victorious, it's better than gold in heaven.

Questions and Prayer:

What kind of trials are you going through right now? Can you see God working in them? Pray today that God would give you the strength to endure and purify your faith through the test.

BE TRANSFORMED

Read: Romans 12:1-2

We are not to be conformed to the world. Imagine a lump of clay and a steel mold. We are told not to be conformed to that mold. We are not to let the world conform us to its ways. Why? It's because the world is filled with unsaved people who live their lives void of God's Word.

We are not to be conformed by the unsaved world filled with people who are doing their own thing. Rather, we are to be transformed. "Transformed" is an important word for us to understand as Christians. It comes from the word "metamorphosis" or "morphe." The best example of metamorphosis is the transformation of a caterpillar into a butterfly. The caterpillar crawls to whatever it can find to eat and spins a cocoon. From there, the caterpillar begins a metamorphosis that completely changes its being. It emerges as a butterfly with wings and no longer needs to crawl.

The Bible tells us not to conform to the world but to go through this metamorphosis so we can follow our transformed mind in our thoughts and actions. The transformation is doing the good, acceptable, and perfect will of God.

We go through this metamorphosis in life, which is the salvation of our souls, and walk through the progression of the good, acceptable, and perfect will of God. We begin to grow in the things of God. The Bible says this is our reasonable service. It is reasonable for us, after Jesus died for us, to change our thinking and be conformed into the image He wants us to be rather than the image we want to be.

Questions and Prayer:

How are you different today from the first day you came to Christ? Can your friends and family tell a difference? Ask God to continue to transform and mold you into a new creation.

DEATH WAS REQUIRED

Read: Colossians 3

We are told to seek the things above and to set our minds on them instead of on the things of the earth. Take note of Verse 4 because it will come into play in next week's sessions. When Jesus appears, we are going to appear with Him in glory. The Bible tells us we, not God, are going to take off the old man and put on the new man. This means we are to take off the flesh-dominating person we once were and put on the spirit-dominating person we should be.

Here is the new man and sweet spot of the fruit of the Spirit. Whatever you do in word and deed you must do unto the Lord. If Jesus was present in the room today, how would you act and what would you say? For example, would David have had his encounter with Bathsheba if Jesus was in the room?

Where is Jesus in your heart and life? Because that's what we are talking about. People want to debate the concept of "once saved, always saved," but the bottom line is this: God fixed what was wrong with humanity, but a death was required. Jesus sat at the highest point in heaven, yet He humbled Himself for us. He was born in a humble manger, lived a sinless life, and put up with the schemes of mankind. He was falsely arrested, falsely accused, and wrongfully hung on the cross. God put all our sins and iniquities on Him. Jesus died humiliated because He had to be separated from God.

Jesus had to go into the belly of the earth, where all spiritually dead men and women went, and then God raised Him from the dead. So isn't it reasonable for us to live for that Man, our King, our Master, our Lord and Savior? Yet, to do that, we have to change the way we think. We have to move from who we were to the new person we have become. This is a continuous process and a lifelong journey. We don't change over night.

Questions and Prayer:

Is there a place where Jesus is not allowed in your life? Maybe it's your office, your kitchen or your dorm room. Ask Jesus to invade your empty spaces this week and make you aware of His presence.

SESSION 9

SALVATION OF THE BODY - RESURRECTION

SESSION 9

SALVATION OF THE BODY - RESURRECTION

1 Corinthians 15:42-58

⁴² SO ALSO IS THE RESURRECTION OF THE DEAD. THE BODY IS SOWN IN CORRUPTION, IT IS RAISED IN INCORRUPTION. ⁴³ IT IS SOWN IN DISHONOR, IT IS RAISED IN GLORY. IT IS SOWN IN WEAKNESS, IT IS RAISED IN POWER. ⁴⁴ IT IS SOWN A NATURAL BODY, IT IS RAISED A SPIRITUAL BODY. THERE IS A NATURAL BODY, AND THERE IS A SPIRITUAL BODY. ⁴⁵ AND SO IT IS WRITTEN, "THE FIRST MAN ADAM BECAME A LIVING BEING." THE LAST ADAM BECAME A LIFE-GIVING SPIRIT. ⁴⁶ HOWEVER, THE SPIRITUAL IS NOT FIRST, BUT THE NATURAL, AND AFTERWARD THE SPIRITUAL. ⁴⁷ THE FIRST MAN WAS OF THE EARTH, MADE OF DUST; THE SECOND MAN IS THE LORD FROM HEAVEN. ⁴⁸ AS WAS THE MAN OF DUST, SO ALSO ARE THOSE WHO ARE MADE OF DUST; AND AS IS THE HEAVENLY MAN, SO ALSO ARE THOSE WHO ARE HEAVENLY. ⁴⁹ AND AS WE HAVE BORNE THE IMAGE OF THE MAN OF DUST, WE SHALL ALSO BEAR THE IMAGE OF THE HEAVENLY MAN. ⁵⁰ NOW THIS I SAY, BRETHREN, THAT FLESH AND BLOOD CANNOT INHERIT THE KINGDOM OF GOD; NOR DOES CORRUPTION INHERIT INCORRUPTION. ⁵¹ BEHOLD, I TELL YOU A MYSTERY: WE SHALL NOT ALL SLEEP, BUT WE SHALL ALL BE CHANGED-- ⁵² IN A MOMENT, IN THE TWINKLING OF AN EYE, AT THE LAST TRUMPET. FOR THE TRUMPET WILL SOUND, AND THE DEAD WILL BE RAISED INCORRUPTIBLE, AND WE SHALL BE CHANGED. ⁵³ FOR THIS CORRUPTIBLE MUST PUT ON INCORRUPTION, AND THIS MORTAL MUST PUT ON IMMORTALITY. ⁵⁴ SO WHEN THIS CORRUPTIBLE HAS PUT ON INCORRUPTION, AND THIS MORTAL HAS PUT ON IMMORTALITY, THEN SHALL BE BROUGHT TO PASS THE SAYING THAT IS WRITTEN: "DEATH IS SWALLOWED UP IN VICTORY." ⁵⁵ "O DEATH, WHERE IS YOUR STING? O HADES, WHERE IS YOUR VICTORY?" ⁵⁶ THE STING OF DEATH IS SIN, AND THE STRENGTH OF SIN IS THE LAW. ⁵⁷ BUT THANKS BE TO GOD, WHO GIVES US THE VICTORY THROUGH OUR LORD JESUS CHRIST. ⁵⁸ THEREFORE, MY BELOVED BRETHREN, BE STEADFAST, IMMOVABLE, ALWAYS ABOUNDING IN THE WORK OF THE LORD, KNOWING THAT YOUR LABOR IS NOT IN VAIN IN THE LORD.

1. The rapture, the return of the Lord, and the resurrection are _____ _____ _____.

2. All of the Saints, from Adam to Able to Abraham, who have died _____ are waiting in heaven for the return of Jesus to the earth. This brings in the final part of salvation, which is the resurrection of our _____.

3. The Saints in heaven are waiting for the _____ of salvation and the end of _____ when Jesus returns to the earth.

4. Our salvation is _____ at the point of our physical death when our spirit and soul are _____ from our bodies.

5. When Jesus returns, He is going to execute _____ and make war with those who took the mark of the _____.

6. There is a body of _____ in heaven who have fallen asleep or died in Christ, and there is another body of _____ here on earth that has not yet died. We are all one family in Christ.

7. Those who are in _____ will return with the Lord, and then the believers on earth will be caught up in the _____ with them, and this is the _____ of the Church.

8. Our mortal and _____ and _____-_____ bodies will be changed in the twinkling of an eye.

9. If we do not believe that Christ was raised from the dead, we are still living in _____.

10. After the resurrection of our bodies, there is no more _____ because the last enemy to be _____ by Jesus Christ is death.

11. Jesus dealt with the _____ of sin in our lives by the renewing of our minds, and God dealt with the _____ of sin by the new birth.

Key Words:

(a) Apostle (b) Faithfulness (c) Sealed (d) Day of the Lord (e) Cleanliness

_____ An event with rewards and blessings for the Saints; Christ coming for His own.

_____ Freedom from worldly corruption or the effects of death.

_____ One sent with a special message or commission in the sense of the Word.

_____ That which is permanent, confirmed and impenetrable to mankind but known to God.

_____ Attribute of God which ensures that He will fulfill His promises and execute His wrath.

Session Answers:

1. one single event

2. physically, bodies

3. completion, death

4. sealed, separated

5. judgment, beast

6. Saints, believers

7. heaven, clouds, rapture

8. corruptible, sin-filled

9. sin

10. death, destroyed

11. power, penalty

Key Word Answers:

d, e, a, c, b

DO YOU LOVE ME?

Read: John 21:15-19

In this story of Peter and Jesus, we don't see what is happening because the English language does not expand the definition of love. In the original language of the Bible, the word "love" has two different meanings.

Jesus asked whether Peter loved Him without boundaries. Jesus wanted to know if Peter "agape" loved Him, which means to unconditionally love Him. Peter said he "phileo" loved Jesus, which meant conditional love. The second time, Jesus was really asking, "Peter, do you love Me unconditionally?" Or "Peter, do you love Me without boundaries?" Peter admitted his love for Jesus had boundaries. You see, we don't get this meaning in our English language because we only see the word "love." We don't see "agape" and "phileo," which brings a whole different meaning to these verses.

So Peter and Jesus go back and forth with this questioning three times. Peter finally says, "Lord You know all things and You knew I was going to deny You, and You knew I was going to be weak and I was." Peter tells Jesus, "You knew You were going to be crucified and I know that You know everything. I see it now, and You told us about it and it happened." The conversation ends with Jesus telling Peter that if he loved Him unconditionally, he would tend to and feed those who are part of Jesus' flock on earth.

Notice how Jesus said something distinctly different to Peter than what we read about with Judas. Jesus told Peter, "You are going to glorify Me with your death," and even told Peter how he would die.

Jesus gave Peter the assurance of salvation. He does the same with us because He loves us! He wants us to know our salvation in the midst of our failures.

Questions and Prayer:

Do you have boundless love for Jesus? Are you sure? Pray today that God would expand His love in your heart.

ONE SINGLE EVENT

Read: Revelation 19

Our salvation is sealed at the point of our physical deaths on earth. That's when our spirit and soul are separated from our bodies. Our bodies will go back to dust in the ground, but our spirits and our souls go into heaven.

When you understand eschatology or end times, the Bible says the angels don't even know when Jesus is going to return. In fact, we read in Matthew 24:36, "But of that day and hour no one knows, not even the angels of heaven, but My Father only." Picture all the Saints, from Adam and Eve to every person after them who was accounted as righteous or found salvation. This brings comfort because all the Saints includes those who are now in heaven, like your parents, grandparents or anyone else who knew Jesus Christ as their Lord and Savior. They have all been waiting in heaven for the day of Christ's return, and today is that day!

There is this amazing voice of a great multitude in heaven praising God with glory, honor, respect and power. We see that the throne of God has four creatures and 24 elders who bow down at the throne. We see the throne speaking back. We see the multitudes saying greatly, now comes the time for the marriage and the union between the Bride of Christ and the Bridegroom who is Christ. After thousands of years, literally millenniums, they are ready for this marriage to occur, and it is here! Our gift of eternal life through Jesus!

This is salvation!

Questions and Prayer:

Can you imagine the day of the Lord? The day of eternal salvation! Pray that God would give you peace in your heart for the day you will meet Him either in the air or through physical death.

PERSONAL DEVOTION SESSION 9 // DAY 3

THE CHURCH IS TAKEN

Read: 1 Thessalonians 4:13-18

I want to review these verses very carefully because there is a lot of debate in the Church about whether or not the rapture and the resurrection are separate from the return of the Lord Jesus.

Regardless of the ongoing debate, I hope to make it very clear to you that the return of the Lord, the rapture and the resurrection are all one single event! The Bible tells us in 1 Thessalonians 4:13-14, "But I do not want you to be ignorant, brethren, concerning those who have fallen asleep, lest you sorrow as others who have no hope. For if we believe that Jesus died and rose again, **even so God will bring with Him** those who sleep in Jesus" (emphasis added). In other words, if we believe in the Gospel plan and we are connected to Jesus, then we are certain God will bring with Him all of the Saints who died in Jesus. Remember, "in Jesus" is a covenant term. Those who are alive and remain will not hinder those who have died and will return with Jesus.

Scripture is very clear that there is a body of believers in heaven who have fallen asleep or who have died in Christ. Also, there is the body of believers on the earth, those who have not yet died.

At the rapture, the Lord returns and those who are in heaven come with Him. When He comes, He comes on the clouds. We will see Saints in the clouds, and we will be caught up in the clouds with them. We also see that there is an angel and a trumpet. All of this activity will be occurring at this event, but most importantly, we are all brought together. The Church on earth with the physical body and the Church in heaven without a physical body will be brought together at this event.

This is the rapture of the Church. It is also the resurrection. It is also the day of the Lord.

Remember there is a cloud, there is Jesus in the cloud, there is the gathering of the Saints in the cloud, and there is the voice of the angel and a trumpet blowing.

Questions and Prayer:

Do you see how the rapture and the day of the Lord are the same? Pray that you would be prepared, alert and ready for the coming of the Lord.

THE GRAND FINALE

Read: 1 Corinthians 15

Sown in corruption, raised in incorruption; Sown in dishonor, raised in glory; Sown in weakness, raised in power; Sown in natural body, raised in spiritual body. We learn that the first man, Adam, became a living being, and the last Adam, Jesus, became a life-giving Spirit.

What is the difference between Adam and Jesus, and the difference in us? The difference is that God was the Father of both Adam and Jesus. There was no human being that made Adam and there was no male seed connected to Jesus. Jesus was born outside of sin. He is the last Adam, meaning, Jesus was the last person God created here on the earth born outside the seed of man.

In Verse 17, we learn if we do not believe that Christ is raised from the dead, we are still living in our sins because the resurrection of Jesus was part of the salvation process.

What we experience at the rapture and resurrection of the Church is that our soul and spirit in heaven are reconnected with a new spiritual body. This is what happened to Jesus 2,000 years before, and it will happen to each of us.

Whenever He returns, we will have our new resurrected bodies. When you look at the big picture, the return of Jesus Christ will be the finale of all things. Death will no longer exist. Do you understand?

The rapture cannot happen before the return of Jesus because where would you place the resurrection of the body for those who are saved during tribulation or those who are saved afterward? It has to be the final act that brings order to everything. When Jesus comes back, He will bring the Saints from heaven with Him and we are all changed and brought together. We will come back to earth with Him. We will then rule and reign with Him for 1,000 years!

Questions and Prayer:

How can you live a life that is prepared, alert and ready for the Day of the Lord? Pray today that the Lord would give you an increased desire to become more like Him.

WE ARE NOW COMPLETE

Read: Philippians 3:18-20

The Bible tells us we must be eagerly awaiting His return. This is the completion of our salvation. It's the completion of who we are in Christ. So our spirits get saved and we become born-again. We are alive to God and become the righteousness of God. The Holy Spirit comes into us and we begin to grow in the things of God through revelation, faith and fruitful actions.

If Jesus does not come back beforehand, we will die. Our spirit and soul will be separated from the body, just like Jesus was for three days and three nights. Jesus was resurrected and reunited with His Spirit and soul so that all the three parts are together again. This event takes place when He comes back for us. Jesus completes the salvation we stand in once we receive our new bodies. This is when our corruptible bodies become incorruptible. Our mortal bodies that can die and get sick become immortal. Our dishonored bodies become honorable. God then gives us our spiritual bodies that will never die.

Through the gift of salvation all three parts of us—spirit, soul and body—are now whole!

Hallelujah! We have a new body!

Questions and Prayer:

Have you shared with someone recently about salvation? Can you find a space in your life to share the good news? Pray today that God would give you boldness to share the good news of salvation with others.

SESSION 10

THE JUDGMENT OF THE CHURCH

THE JUDGMENT OF THE CHURCH

Matthew 11:16-24

¹⁶ BUT TO WHAT SHALL I LIKEN THIS GENERATION? IT IS LIKE CHILDREN SITTING IN THE MARKETPLACES AND CALLING TO THEIR COMPANIONS, ¹⁷ AND SAYING: 'WE PLAYED THE FLUTE FOR YOU, AND YOU DID NOT DANCE; WE MOURNED TO YOU, AND YOU DID NOT LAMENT.' ¹⁸ FOR JOHN CAME NEITHER EATING NOR DRINKING, AND THEY SAY, 'HE HAS A DEMON.' ¹⁹ THE SON OF MAN CAME EATING AND DRINKING, AND THEY SAY, 'LOOK, A GLUTTON AND A WINEBIBBER, A FRIEND OF TAX COLLECTORS AND SINNERS!' BUT WISDOM IS JUSTIFIED BY HER CHILDREN." ²⁰ THEN HE BEGAN TO REBUKE THE CITIES IN WHICH MOST OF HIS MIGHTY WORKS HAD BEEN DONE, BECAUSE THEY DID NOT REPENT: ²¹ "WOE TO YOU, CHORAZIN! WOE TO YOU, BETHSAIDA! FOR IF THE MIGHTY WORKS WHICH WERE DONE IN YOU HAD BEEN DONE IN TYRE AND SIDON, THEY WOULD HAVE REPENTED LONG AGO IN SACKCLOTH AND ASHES. ²² BUT I SAY TO YOU, IT WILL BE MORE TOLERABLE FOR TYRE AND SIDON IN THE DAY OF JUDGMENT THAN FOR YOU. ²³ AND YOU, CAPERNAUM, WHO ARE EXALTED TO HEAVEN, WILL BE BROUGHT DOWN TO HADES; FOR IF THE MIGHTY WORKS WHICH WERE DONE IN YOU HAD BEEN DONE IN SODOM, IT WOULD HAVE REMAINED UNTIL THIS DAY. ²⁴ BUT I SAY TO YOU THAT IT SHALL BE MORE TOLERABLE FOR THE LAND OF SODOM IN THE DAY OF JUDGMENT THAN FOR YOU."

1. The greatest man born of a woman during the time of Jesus was _____ _____ _____ and the reason was because John was a prophet and he had the _____ to actually walk with Jesus Christ.

2. To our knowledge, John never performed any _____, yet he was the greatest in the kingdom. John's gift was that he was completely void of _____ _____ and whole-hearted toward God.

3. The world evaluates success by _____ and _____, but God evaluates success in John the Baptist and His Son, Jesus Christ.

4. In our _____ of time, we have more privilege than anyone before us because we have the _____ of Jesus Christ, the Holy Spirit and the _____ _____.

5. We do not see things the way God sees them because His _____ and _____ are not the same as ours, and this is why we must _____ His ways and thoughts in His Word.

6. In our dispensation of time, those who have seen and _____ the anointing, but do not respond in _____ and _____ will receive a harsher judgment than those who have never heard the Gospel message or seen the anointing.

7. The Holy Spirit draws people to Him through the millions of people who _____, _____ and _____ the fruit of the Gospel message.

8. We must comprehend the _____ of our great relationship with Jesus and clearly understand that if we walk away from Him it will be even more _____ for us in the end.

9. Our relationship with Jesus should be _____, but what is missing today in Christianity is _____ _____ and the expectation that is upon us as Christians.

10. Our piles of righteous works are either done for the glory of God or they are done for the _____ _____ _____. The pile is judged by fire, and the works done for mankind are burnt away. Whatever is left are the _____ we take with us into eternity.

11. When we get to heaven our blessings are _____, and this is who we will be _____. We must formulate this into our lives here on earth.

12. We are saved from _____ and brought into a family where God is our Father and _____ is our eternal destiny. What a privilege we stand in by knowing Jesus Christ as our Lord and Savior!

Key Words:

(a) Anoint   (b) Dispensation of Grace   (c) Alms   (d) Nazarite   (e) Eternal Life

_____   Formal consecration for a sacred purpose; to be set apart from others.

_____   Bound by a vow of a specific kind to be of service only to God.

_____   Money or food given freely to relieve the poor.

_____   Not to be confused with mere endless existence for the saved and unsaved.

_____   Period not bound to the obedience of law but to the acceptance or rejection of Christ.

Session Answers:

1. John the Baptist, privilege

2. miracles, worldly things

3. glitz, glamour

4. dispensation, revelation, new birth

5. thoughts, ways, learn

6. experienced, faith, action

7. teach, preach, reveal

8. gravity, tragic

9. joyful, godly fear

10. approval of man, blessings

11. sealed, forever

12. damnation, heaven

Key Word Answers:

a, d, c, e, b

THE HEART OF JESUS

Read: John 12:1-8

In these verses we learn Mary took the money she had saved to buy fragrant oil that she used to anoint the feet of Jesus for His burial. The cost of that oil was about a year's worth of wages for the average person back then. It cost about three hundred denarii, and the average wage was one denarii a day. When Mary poured the ointment on Jesus' feet, Judas wanted to know why Mary had wasted the oil.

When you back up from this story, it's important to understand that Judas was with Jesus and His ministry for three and a half years. Judas saw virtue and love in Jesus, and he saw how Jesus was connected to God. Judas watched Jesus work miracles, heal broken lives, and bring people back from the dead. He witnessed all these things, yet nothing changed fundamentally in him. The capstone is Judas felt Jesus was not worth the fragrant oil. This is what Judas meant when he questioned Mary's actions. Judas wanted to know why Mary had wasted the oil on Jesus.

Doesn't the mindset of Judas make you recoil? That someone would dare to say the fragrant oil was wasted on our Lord and Savior? Especially when Jesus was about to go to the cross for us! But that was the heart of Judas. He never elevated Jesus to the position of Lord and Savior. Judas never made the migration of placing Jesus above himself as the Creator and authority over his life. He never looked to Jesus as the One who would die for him. As a result, Judas was upset and indignant about how the ministry money was being spent. Stop and ask yourself, how many Judases do we have in the earth today, people who put money or things above Jesus?

Questions and Prayer:

Is there anything in your life that may be above Jesus? Could it be your money, time or other relationships? Ask God to reveal those things to you and to give you the grace to reposition them in your life to make Him first, always.

WHAT DID YOU EXPECT?

Read: Matthew 11

John the Baptist and his ministry were located about five miles from the city of Jerusalem. Those who wanted to hear him preach had to walk there. The area where John lived was in the wilderness, and for all intents and purposes, John was homeless. He lived in a tent and off the land. He was a Nazarite who didn't shave his beard or cut his hair, and his diet was limited to certain things.

When people traveled out to the wilderness to see John, Jesus would ask them what they expected to see. "Did you expect to see a preacher in a flashy new suit? Did you expect to see someone who is all glitz and glamour?" In other words, what Jesus was asking was if they expected to see someone who was worldly successful—someone who would shine and was well polished. Jesus wanted to know what they expected when they went out to see John the Baptist. In a way, Jesus was poking at the values and mindset of the crowd when He asks them what they expected.

In the world's eyes, John was the opposite of success, but Jesus tells them John was the greatest man born of a woman up to this time. Why is that? It's because John was preparing people for God's salvation. He was preparing men and women for Jesus. John was revealing Jesus to them.

God uses people and things like this to confound us. He uses shabby people when we expect glitz and glamour. He uses weakness to reveal His strength. He uses people who look the exact opposite of what we expect. In fact, Jesus said to the people that they were expecting great worldly glitz and glamour because that is how they evaluate success. Jesus told them how He gave them something to react to and they didn't react! They should have been joyful at some of the messages taught, and mournful at others, but the people did not react. In other words, there was the opportunity of salvation for everyone, but the people ignored it.

Questions and Prayer:

Has God ever brought something unexpected to you? How did you react? Today, ask God to reveal the things He is using to shape and mold you.

THE GRAVITY OF THINGS

Read: Luke 12:40-50

These verses open up with the warning to be ready because we don't know when we will meet the Son of God. Of course, Jesus is talking about His return, but let me caution you: each of us will meet the Son of God when our hearts stop beating! Amen. You may not need the rapture to come face-to-face with Jesus.

In Luke, we learn that the wise steward is found doing what he is supposed to be doing when His Lord returns. We are doing what we're supposed to be doing when we are fruitful. Receiving revelation knowledge and walking and acting upon your faith is being fruitful.

Can you understand the gravity and weight of doing the work of God and living your life for Him? We are told that if the servant who has a relationship with and knows his Master turns back and lives like the world by walking away from the things of God, then God will appoint him his portion with the unbeliever.

In Verse 47, we learn that the servant who knows God's will but does not do God's will, shall be beaten or judged more harshly. Those who have much will be asked to do more. We learn there is a requirement on us who walk in the dispensation of time that we are living. We must understand it is a privilege to walk in the new birth.

Questions and Prayer:

What have you been entrusted with? Would you consider it much or little? Do you feel a responsibility for the things you have been entrusted? Ask God to help you manage your gifts, talents, and calling to the best of your ability.

THE PILE BEFORE YOU

Read: 1 Corinthians 3:8-11

Paul tells us that he has laid a foundation of faith, and like him, we are to build upon that foundation of faith in Jesus as our Lord and Savior.

In Verse 12 we are given six elements: gold, silver, precious stone, wood, hay and stubble. When we place our faith in Jesus and salvation is our foundation, our house is built on all six of these elements. Paul said when the Lord returns each one of us will have a pile of these elements before us. Wood, hay and stubble define the righteous acts done in faith but for the approval of man. Gold, silver and precious stones represent things of eternal value done entirely for the glory of God.

Fire will come down and burn up the wood, hay and stubble. It takes it all away. What's left? The things of value, which are gold, silver and precious stones. Christians are not judged by our sins—we are judged by our righteous works done in faith and love with a pure heart for the Lord. Whether our actions were done with the right intent or whether they were done to be seen of men, all of them will be heaped on this pile.

The judgment of our actions will determine whether or not we will carry them into eternity. Actions done for the glory of man will be burned before we go into everlasting life with Jesus. There will be no eternal rewards for actions done for the approval of man. We carry gold, silver and precious stones into eternity.

Questions and Prayer:

Are your acts of righteousness done for recognition by people, or for recognition by the heavenly Father? Pray that God would change your heart and make your intentions for His glory to be seen and given by God.

REWARDS OF VALUE

Read: Matthew 6

In Matthew 6, we are told charitable deeds are things Christians are called to do. These deeds are giving alms and giving of our time and services to others. The Bible teaches us that righteous acts of giving can be done in two ways. A deed of faith is done with a pure heart to God. It is not done for the approval of man. The deeds of faith we perform on earth will be our rewards in heaven. We are given our reward on earth when we do charitable deeds for the glory of man. These deeds become wood, hay and stubble in the eyes of God.

The difference between these two types of charitable deeds is faith. When I have faith in God, I don't need the approval of man. I am acting for God, and God sees it and honors my actions. That is all that matters to Christians. Man's glory means nothing.

Giving, praying and fasting are actions we are all commanded to do; it's part of the Word and comes from the renewing of our minds. It's part of growing in the things of God. But remember, we can do them with the intention of the glory of man. If you are seeking man's approval and want to be seen by and rewarded by men, that is not faith. Charitable acts done in secret only for God to see are actions blessed by God.

Yes, we do stand today in a perpetual place of salvation, but what we are judged by is our fruit or our light. The good deeds we do here on earth and how we do them will determine our seats in heaven. Just remember: there are cheap seats and good seats, but then there are front row seats! Which seat are you striving for?

This process takes place upon the return of the Lord. And believe me, each of us will stand before Him alone. When fire comes down to burn your pile of wood, hay and stubble, will there be any gold, silver and precious stones left for you to take into eternity? What remains is the status of who you will be forever. Saints, our rewards are built upon our actions while we are living on earth.

Questions and Prayer:

Check the motives of your heart. Are they with God in mind or with you in mind? Pray that God would take away the selfish desires of your heart and give you a heart like His.